JOURNEY THROUGH
THE WEALD

Journey Through the Weald

by

Ben Darby

with photographs by the author

ROBERT HALE · LONDON

© Ben Darby 1986
First published in Great Britain 1986

Robert Hale Limited
Clerkenwell House
Clerkenwell Green
London EC1R 0HT

British Library Cataloguing in Publication Data

Darby, Ben
  Journey through the Weald.
  1. Weald (England)—Description and travel
  —Guide-books
  I. Title
  914.22′5   DA670.W43

ISBN 0-7090-2586-6

Photoset in North Wales by
Derek Doyle & Associates, Mold, Clwyd.
Printed in Great Britain by
St Edmundsbury Press, Bury St Edmunds, Suffolk.
Bound by Woolnough Bookbinding Limited.

Contents

Acknowledgements

If I were to thank personally all those who have helped me write this book, I should need another chapter. Librarians have spared no trouble in looking up and verifying facts. Local authorities have suggested, and then promptly sent me, regional publications. The Countryside Commission, Nature Conservancy Council and Forestry Commission have all guided me from their particular conservation standpoints.

Photographic printers Messrs Taylors, of Hove, have made certain that I should have quality prints from my negatives.

My sincere thanks to my publishers who, not once, but many times, have held back my deadline.

Finally, I am deeply grateful to my wife Doreen for doing all the typing at the last minute and for checking the manuscript. And then for selecting the title of the book, *Journey Through The Weald*.

Illustrations

Maps

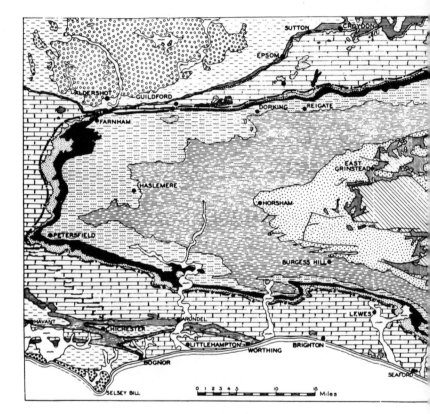

Geological map of the Weald

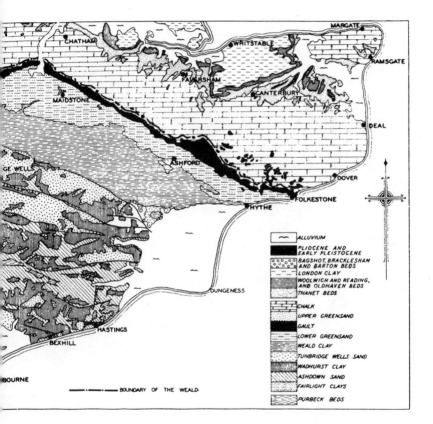

CHATHAM •   • WHITSTABLE   MARGATE

RAMSGATE •

FAVERSHAM

• MAIDSTONE   • CANTERBURY

• DEAL

GE WELLS   ASHFORD •

• DOVER

• FOLKESTONE
• HYTHE

DUNGENESS

	ALLUVIUM
	PLIOCENE AND EARLY PLEISTOCENE
	BAGSHOT, BRACKLESHAM AND BARTON BEDS
	LONDON CLAY
	WOOLWICH AND READING, AND OLDHAVEN BEDS
	THANET BEDS
	CHALK
	UPPER GREENSAND
	GAULT
	LOWER GREENSAND
	WEALD CLAY
	TUNBRIDGE WELLS SAND
	WADHURST CLAY
	ASHDOWN SAND
	FAIRLIGHT CLAYS
	PURBECK BEDS

HASTINGS •
• BEXHILL

BOURNE   ——— BOUNDARY OF THE WEALD

1

The Weald

What is the Weald? Where is the Weald? Many people who actually live there could not answer these questions. Geological and geographical textbooks explain that it is the name of the great valley lying between the North Downs and the South Downs. Strictly speaking, this is true but it is a vast over-simplification. It suggests a large green bowl sloping down from surrounding hills. Nothing could be further from the truth. The landscape is extraordinarily varied within the confines of the two downland ranges. There are tall hills and deep valleys, high ridges and flat lands and a lot of rivers. Many of the hills are much higher than the enclosing downs.

The structure of the Weald is a never-ending source of fascination to geologists, who continually study it. An eminent geologist, the late Sir Lawrence Dudley Stamp, called it 'one of the most fascinating regions of all Europe' and pointed out that 'It is slow to yield up all its secrets.' We need to know something about this geological structure if we are to understand and appreciate the intricate and often puzzling Wealden countryside.

Geologists believe that about 120 million years ago a great lake or delta plain, or perhaps a mixture of lake and plain, lay where the Weald lies now. What we now call the British Isles formed part of the landmass of Europe. The water of the lake or semi-lake may have been fresh or brackish, or partly both, or alternately one or the other, changing as the long ages passed. Sands and mud formed the bed of the lake. There were certainly long periods of fresh water, for we know that in it lived a freshwater snail called *Viviparus Paludina*. This creature drifted down into the mud, and its shells built up into masses and formed dense limestone, a form of marble which we shall discuss more fully later.

Luxuriant vegetation clothed the marshy lands around the lake. It included conifers, palm-like trees and giant ferns. Huge reptiles

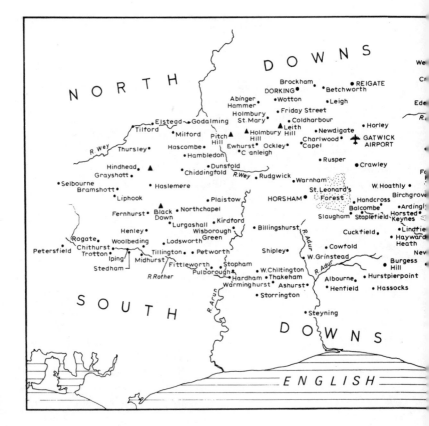

The Weald

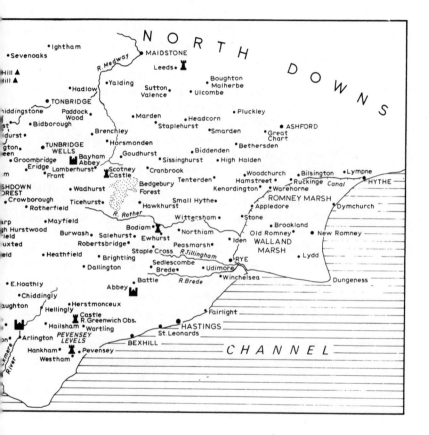

roamed the landscape, browsing on the lush foliage. They were probably peaceable creatures and not the snarling brutes portrayed by the cinema.

By about 65 million years ago the land had sunk. The sea washed over most of the area which eventually became Britain. The Wealden lake, swamps and surrounding countryside completely disappeared. So did the monsters, but that may have been a coincidence since they were disappearing on a world scale. Some scientists believe that the geological change and the disappearance of the monsters were gradual. Some think both were due to a sudden cosmic cataclysm. Scientists are persistent investigators, and one day they will be able to tell us the true story.

Fresh muds and sands accumulated through the period that followed. Then an entirely new substance began to drift through the water. It built up on the old lake bed to a depth of a thousand feet or more. This new substance marked the beginning of the Wealden landscape as we know it today. It was chalk. In the period which began about 20 million years ago the sea retreated and left a giant dome of this chalk open to the skies. It covered virtually the whole of what we now call south-east England and northern France. But the wind and the weather got to work on it, helped at least once more by the sea, and they wore away the top and centre of the dome, leaving only two long, curving stumps which we call the North and the South Downs. On the map they look like a suppressed oval, open-ended on the east side. Between them lies what we now call the Weald, the central part of the ancient lake. Today it is richly clad in verdant vegetation, but in places sandstone rock thrusts through in massive outcrops, relics of the oldest part of the primeval lake bed.

The great variations of the landscape are due to the extraordinary diversities of the soil, themselves the result of the gradual geological build-up on the great lake or swamp. It is nevertheless an entity, a single countryside. The geological map on pages x–xi clearly illustrate this. Note how different types of soil follow one another in a series of ovals within the enclosing oval of chalk. First there is a belt of light and sometimes sandy soil immediately next to the chalk downs. Geologists call it upper greensand. This belt is very narrow, and under the eastern part of the North Downs it is scarcely noticeable at all. Next comes gault, an obstinate clay. This is succeeded by lower greensand, fairly wide in most places, very extensive in the west, and often so truly sandy that if you took off your shoes and shut your eyes you might believe yourself to be on the seashore. Both upper and lower greensand contain grains of a greenish mineral which have given these soils their name, though it is quite likely that you will never come across any suggestion of green. On the lower greensand you will find some of the most beautiful scenery not only in the Weald but in England. After this stretch comes a band of Weald clay, sometimes broad, sometimes narrow, very sticky in wet weather, iron hard in hot.

Then you come to the centre of the Weald, its core, and its oldest soils, a mixture of what the geologists call Ashdown sands and Tunbridge Wells sands, liberally bespattered with Wadhurst clay. It compromises three sections: a heavily wooded tract called the Forest Ridge, Ashdown Forest and a high extensive area at its edge which ends at Romney Marsh and sandstone cliffs facing the English Channel. Though the three sections are of the same geological structure, they differ in other respects. They are often called collectively the High Weald, but I have presumed to use the term to cover the big eastern area only, and for the other two I use the names by which they are more generally known. Confusion sometimes ensues when you refer to the 'High Weald' because, though it is certainly high, many districts in the Weald are much higher.

The great diversity of soil has produced a comparable diversity in vegetation. Plants which grow in one region will not grow, or not as well, in another. This applies both to wild plants and trees and to cultivated agricultural produce and cultivated forestry timber. Birds, animals, insects and even reptiles also vary with the different soil and vegetation.

What the geological map does not show is altitude. Excellent Ordnance Survey maps indicate heights by contour lines. Some maps do so by means of contrasting colours. The best way to gain a true impression of what the Weald looks like is by means of a model of the region. Then you see at a glance the hills, the flat lands, the surrounding chalk downs and also the shape of the region. The Weald we know today is narrow and very long. It stretches ninety miles from the eastern end of Romney Marsh to the edge of the downland west of Petersfield and Farnham. It is about thirty-six-miles at its widest, from Pevensey Bay to a point north-east of Sevenoaks and north-west of Maidstone. It comprises all Sussex apart from the South Downs and the coastal plain between Shoreham and Chichester Harbour, a big chunk of Kent, all of Surrey south of the North Downs, and a small area of Hampshire. The hand of man now lies firmly upon the entire region. There are extensive areas of wild countryside, but it is controlled and managed wilderness. If management were withdrawn, the land would soon become truly wild and impassable.

It seems likely that man began to appear in the Weald earlier than 40,000 BC, and these shadowy, far off lower palaeolithic people have left some slight traces. They must have led excessively uncomfortable lives, for the Weald had become a frigid tundra in the grip of the Ice Age. The ice came no further south than the Thames Valley but its influence certainly did. Life was possible in this harsh and hostile Weald, but only just. The Ice Age lasted some 600,000 years, relieved by occasional warmer periods, until 8,000 to 9,000 BC, when the ice finally relented. What caused this cold climatic upheaval is yet another problem the scientists seek to solve.

We know little about the palaeolithics and not a great deal more about their successors who arrived in the south-east about 10,000 BC. They are called the mesolithic people because they stand between the peoples of the old stone age and the new, between the palaeolithic and the neolithic. They were nomadic hunters and food-gatherers but they established some settlements in the higher and sandier regions of the Weald. The neolithic people arrived between 4,000 and 3,000 BC. They were our first farmers and mostly stuck to the Downs. Below lay a vast and swampy jungle, which is what the Weald had become, and the neoliths made hunting forays into it. They used stone weapons and implements which have survived in large number. Some are highly polished and beautiful.

About 1,800 BC a different and more civilized people reached Britain. They brought with them sophisticated weapons, implements and utensils made of bronze, an alloy of copper and tin. These Bronze Age people made their homes chiefly on the chalk hills, but there is evidence that they also settled on the higher lands of the Weald in fair numbers. Mr J.R. Armstrong, the historian, says that, 'There are some grounds for assuming that the central Weald was more generally settled and utilized in this period than it has previously been supposed.'

About 600 to 500 BC another new type of people arrived in Britain. At first they came in small groups but eventually they came in waves. They were vigorous, warlike, talented and artistic, and they brought with them weapons and implements made of a material much stronger than bronze. The newcomers were the Celts, and the material they brought was iron. Like the neoliths and the Bronze Age people, they concentrated their settlements on the Downs, where they built earthworks in abundance, often superimposing them on the structures of the Bronze Age people and the neoliths. They constructed powerful forts on the hilltops, and their burial mounds, the typical Celtic round barrows, are so numerous that it is scarcely an exaggeration to say that on the Downs you are hardly ever out of sight of one. They also laid out their farms in an orderly fashion, and you can still see the traces of their characteristic square fields. They shored up the steep slopes in terraces to provide level surfaces for cultivation.

They disliked the forbidding Weald, to them a place of darkness and peril, but nevertheless they made organized expeditions into it. They discovered that within its hidden depths lay iron, and they were not slow to set about mining it. They hacked out tracks through the jungle to the mines, and it is likely that parties of miners set up temporary living places nearby, like prospectors' camps. Some of these rough encampments in the less unlikeable places may have developed into permanent settlements. The iron was carried out of the forest along the tracks and up the steep sides of the Downs to their hill villages.

The Romans probably knew about this iron before they invaded Britain in the first century. They encouraged the Celts to carry on, and they drove better roads to the mining sites so that it became a straightforward matter to transport iron both to the coast and to Londinium. The Romans, however, like their predecessors, had no love for the Weald, which they called Sylva Anderida. They made no attempt to clear it, still less to settle in it, but their intrepid engineers drove their uncompromising highways across it with the single purpose of linking one specific place with another. Often the minor roads from the iron mines joined these major highways. Posting stations established on the main arteries called for permanent habitations, and pleasant country villas were some-times built in the neighbourhood, but beyond these small incursions of civilization into the wilderness the Romans did nothing to tame the Weald.

The Saxons gradually took over Britain when the Legions had to fall back across Europe to defend Rome. They were quite dissimilar to any of their predecessors. They did not fear the Weald, which now for the first time began to feel the definite impress of man. They entirely lacked the civilizing touch of the Romans and ignored the Romans' first-class system of communi-cations and administration. But they brought with them strong, though crude, implements and, shunning the downland hilltops, they began to make clearances in the forest, establishing first the steading and then the temple to whatever gods they were worshipping. The clearing gradually extended and the Saxon village developed. Fields were carved out for crops, cattle and pigs. It was work which demanded the utmost in physical endurance and tenacity, but the Saxons were a tenacious lot. Bit by bit they felled the trees, wrenched away lesser but tangled vegetation, and on the soils which had built up on the floor of the primeval lake they grew corn for their bread and grass for their cattle.

The villages live on. Though their architecture is now vastly different, their names survive, frequently almost identical with the original; the ring of true Saxon words reaches us across fifteen centuries. The last syllable of these place-names is more often than not an accurate guide to the Saxon Wealden landscape. There are the -dens, the earliest of the clearings and most often found in the eastern, Kentish Weald, as in Tenterden. Then there are the -hursts, hilltop spinneys; the -hams, farmsteads or pastures by water, usually a river; and the -tons, enclosures. In everyday speech it is not uncommon, even today, to hear among older Wealden countrymen a word or two of authentic Saxon; for instance, 'Git holt of ...' instead of 'Get hold of ...' and 'shep' instead of 'sheep'.

Finally there is the Weald itself. The Saxons gave us the name. They called the great forest jungle 'Andredswald' or 'Andreds-

weald'. 'Wald' is the Saxon word for woodland. The preface 'andred' could mean forest, but the word may be Celtic, and if so this
would be one of the very rare cases of Saxon merging with Celt. The
similarity with the Roman Sylva Anderida seems obvious, but it
would be unwise to assume any association. *The Oxford Dictionary
of English Place Names* suggests that 'Andred' could have been the
name of a place, or perhaps the name of a person.

The Saxon villages scattered about the Weald suffered little or no
interference from the Normans, who arrived on the Wealden coast
in 1066, and the Saxon farmers were left to their established pattern.
More houses and churches of stone gradually appeared in place of
existing timber buildings but there was no dramatic upheaval in the
countryside. The Normans knew when to leave well alone.

The clearances which the Saxons made in the Weald were considerable in themselves but compared with the vast extent of the
forest they were as nothing. What eventually led to its wholesale
clearance, almost to its complete destruction, was iron, which the
Saxons ignored, if they ever noticed it at all. It lay forgotten under
the roots of the forest. The Celtic quarries became overgrown and
choked. But somebody suddenly remembered it in the thirteenth
century, and the iron industry set out on a road to modest revival.
There are few records of this, but one thing we know: in 1266 King
Henry III made a grant of a penny on every load of iron taken to
Lewes. New and more efficient smelting methods from France gave
it a big impetus in the fifteenth century, and in the two succeeding
centuries it boomed. The trees of ancient Andredsweald crashed
down at a hectic rate to provide charcoal fuel for the insatiable
furnaces, and there came a time when all could see that the supply
could not last much longer. That problem was solved elsewhere,
however. Both coal and iron were discovered in close proximity in
the North. The industry moved from one end of the country to the
other.

Nature and agriculture healed the scars of Andredsweald, which,
though it is no longer anything like the dense forest it was once, has
yet become again one of the most heavily wooded regions in the
country.

But we shall begin our exploration of the Weald in an area almost
without trees. This bare countryside is the Romney Marsh.

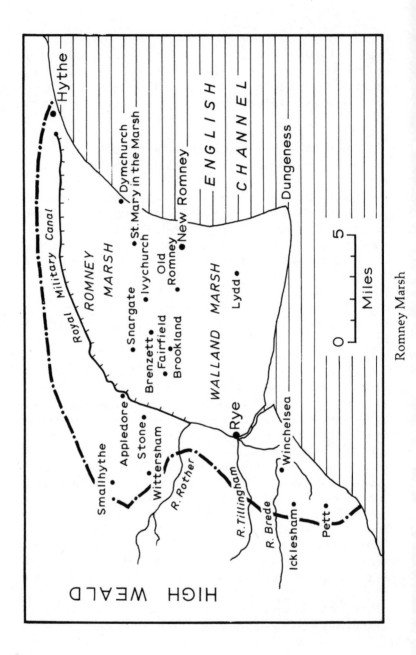

Romney Marsh

2

Romney Marsh

Romney Marsh has a strange, elusive quality and an undramatic but haunting beauty. Most people find it enchanting, some find it eerie, and everybody finds it indefinable. The Reverend R.H. Barham shared with others the difficulty of capturing in words the character of Romney Marsh but overcame it by investing the region with a continental status of its own. In his *Ingoldsby Legends* he wrote: 'The world according to the best geographers is divided into Europe, Asia, Africa, America and Romney Marsh.' Barham knew the area well. He was born not far off, in Canterbury, in 1788, and for four years he was parson of two marshland parishes, Snargate and Warehorne.

'Romney Marsh' is an all-embracing term. Romney Marsh itself comprises about 24,000 acres, less than half the area, some 58,860 acres, which its name is loosely made to cover. The rest is made up of Walland Marsh, Denge Marsh, the Rother Levels and various other levels, and you do not know when you have passed from one to another. Marshmen have simply dubbed the whole lot comprehensively 'the Marsh'.

When you stand upon its levels, you feel none of the monotony which extensive flatness usually conveys. This is because you are never out of sight of hills. The eye, travelling over the flats, reaches distant hills in all but one direction. They form a long crescent round the Marsh west, north and east, and southward lies the sea. Villages and towns are few. Most are ancient, some are very beautiful, and the low-hung houses cling close to the earth, often protected by belts of giant white willows which break the force of the savage winds sweeping in from the south-west and south-east. An extraordinarily large number of churches rise from the flat land. They seem to have grown there, and you come upon then unexpectedly, isolated by stream or channel or out upon the flats, and when you do you are suddenly aware of the deep loneliness of the strange region.

Marshmen who lived, like Barham, in the eighteenth century were strongly influenced by the remoteness of their countryside; they were withdrawn and insular. They were also suspicious when visited by foreigners, which meant anybody not a marshman. This is true to some extent even today, but there has been a great opening up since the end of the Second World War.

Until the end of the 1930s the Marsh was predominantly grass, supporting great flocks of sheep and big herds of cattle. It was a wonderful sight, and on 1 September 1823 it threw William Cobbett into ecstasies of delight, most unusual for this dour radical.

The flocks and herds immense [he wrote in *Rural Rides*, his classic diary about his horseback journeys through England]. The sheep are of a breed that takes its name from the marsh. They are called Romney Marsh sheep. Very pretty and large ... The faces of these sheep are white; and, indeed, the whole sheep is as white as a piece of blotting paper. The wool does not look dirty and oily like that of other sheep. The cattle appear to be all of the Sussex breed. Red, loose-limbed, and, they say, a great deal better than the Devonshire ... With cattle of this kind and with sheep such as I have spoken of before, this marsh abounds in every part of it; and the sight is most beautiful.

Romney Marsh was one of the country's highest invasion risks in 1940, but when it came to evacuation, it was not women and children who went first, though they were in no way neglected or forgotten. It was the sheep. This vast reservoir of food had to be saved for Britain and denied to the Nazis. Sheep-train specials took 85,000 sheep off the Marsh and deposited them at points from which they were distributed to various farms in the kingdom. When the threat of invasion receded, the spreading marshland was left empty and the nation was crying out for food. It would have been impossible to restock it with sheep and cattle and no such attempt was made. Instead a new type of farming was introduced, already popularized by Sir George Stapledon of Aberystwyth University and widely practised elsewhere. He called it ley farming. A ley is temporary pasture, as opposed to permanent pasture. It forms part of a crop rotation, and you might therefore call it arable grass. It is sown like any other crop, and after a certain term of years it is ploughed and the land drilled with something else. In the meantime other crops of grass, new leys, are coming on in other fields. Sir George stressed that the scientific practice of ley farming would produce a lot more food per acre, and in a very short time he was proved abundantly right.

So the ploughs bit into the rich and ancient pastures of the Marsh, brought to a state of great fertility by centuries of manuring by the sheep. Marshmen predicted crop disaster through drowning, since the Marsh was subject to flooding and anyway was always more than a little damp, to say the least. They were wrong. Great crops of corn and roots resulted. Marsh farmers stubbornly continued to detest the change, but worse was to come. 'Foreigners' arrived from Lincolnshire, buying land which was cheaper than the flat land of their own country and generally more fertile; and they planted bulbs. Tulips and daffodils appeared where the famous Romney Marsh sheep once grazed. Marshmen were scandalized, but the new pattern has endured. Today the Marsh is mixed arable and ley pasture. It carries more sheep per acre than it used to, and owing to improved drainage, sheep do not have to be moved in winter to higher land. That was once a traditional scene: the flocks of sheep travelling with their shepherds away from the wet lowlands slowly up to the drier lands inland, often many miles away. A certain number of sheep still winter away from the Marsh, but today they go in lorries.

The new farming has not banished the old beauty, the constantly changing light, the cloud shadows that slide down the hills and dapple the flat land and glide away over the sea, the willows and reeds that grow beside the dykes and other water-courses. The sea is almost always to be seen and frequently heard. Sometimes, however, on calm, white days, when the sky is covered with thin, translucid cloud, it becomes invisible to anybody standing a mile or so back from the shore. White sky merges with white sea and there is no horizon, no line of demarcation. On such days a stranger will rub his eyes in disbelief as a ship floats by apparently high above you in the air.

The sea is often well above you when you stand on the flats, particularly when the spring tides are running. Strong sea walls have been built to keep it out, and these have become an integral part of the Marsh scene. Your view of the sea is momentarily blocked as you make your way towards some section of the high wall, and it is with considerable astonishment that you suddenly discover the waves within a few yards and possibly on a level with your head. Cobbett experienced this sudden discovery of sea and shore. Having made his way to New Romney, 'To my great surpise I found myself upon the sea beach ... Never was I so much surprised as when I saw a sail.' Plans were made in the last war to breach the wall and flood the Marsh if invasion looked certain. A similar scheme was drawn up in 1804 to deter the forces of Napoleon.

The geological history of Romney Marsh, though practically contemporary compared with the structure of the Weald as a whole, is nevertheless of the highest interest. The low crescent of hills which now curtains the Marsh from the higher ground is the remains of cliffs which once enclosed a great bay. The bay gradually silted up, creating a rich, alluvial soil, but this did not happen in one progressive process. The sea has advanced and retreated, the land has risen and fallen, in a series of see-saw movements. Once a forest stood there. Primitive communities made their homes there. The sea came in, drowned the trees and retreated, and the bay became a morass of mud and tangled vegetation. All the time, silt was building up from rivers, three in particular, the Rother, the Brede and the Tillingham, all still there and still bringing down slit.

The strange ups and downs of the land have been ingeniously tabulated by Mr Walter J.C. Murray in his excellent book *Romney Marsh*, which everybody planning to explore the Marsh should read. His researches show that the earth was seventy feet above the present level twelve thousand years ago, and that since AD 500 it has been suffering one of its depressions and now lies below sea-level at high tide.

Man had begun to take a strong controlling hand by the time this last subsidence began. The Romans brought their engineering genius into play and built the first sea wall where the great

Dymchurch Wall runs today. The Church, from Canterbury, instituted well thought-out drainage and protection schemes. As the sea was pushed back, so the silt built up, and presently the towns and villages which had developed along estuaries and inlets were left high and dry, although the sea lapped hungrily at the nearby defensive works, ready to wash in the minute a breach occurred.

Grass grew, and in the course of time the Marsh became the most famous grazing ground in the world. The forest and the swamp were no more than boggy legends, only half believed. But the big mechanical implements of modern agriculture and drainage have brought them very much to mind, if not to life. The great ploughs, ditchers and dredgers cut through the silt like butter, but occasionally they are jarred to a shocked standstill. Workers in the early days of deep cultivation were constantly astounded when this happened, but today's drivers know well enough what has immobilized their machines. They have struck a prehistoric tree trunk and it has to be dug out. Then it lies on the surface of the rich earth, massive, black as ebony, hard as rock. Marshmen call these ancient trees 'moor oaks', a reminder that the term 'moor' does not always mean tracts of heath, bracken, pine and rock. It may equally well mean stretches of flat and damp pasture. Such an area is called 'the moors' near Roxwell, in Essex. Parts of the big Somerset wetlands are known as 'the moors', and also in Somerset there is, of course, Sedgemoor. Similarly, there is Shirley Moor at the north-west corner of Romney Marsh.

The price of this ultra-efficiency in drainage and deep cultivation, leading to an impressive increase in food production, has been a big decrease in wildlife, particularly birds, which thrived on the permanent and damp pastures and the waterways. They found an ideal habitat in the streams, dykes (pronounced 'diks' by country people) and the wider but slow-moving courses into which the smaller waterways emptied themselves, and still do, though more quickly now.

We have noticed the reeds and the willows by the water's edge, but these are a mere fraction of what they were. The vegetation was often thick and overhanging. In its deep recesses many different species of wildfowl found refuge, while down in the slow-moving water the dabbling types of waterbirds could find food among the roots of aquatic plants which, themselves, were often rare and always varied and interesting. They were decimated in the widening of the waterways, and powerful pumps thrust forward more quickly the passage of the waters.

It would be wrong to suppose that the entire marsh has been sacrificed to intensive agriculture. Just as the old beauty remains, so does the wildlife, though on a much reduced scale. The Nature Conservancy Council guards a Site of Special Scientific Interest at the western end of the Marsh, and there are nature reserves at Dungeness and Rye Harbour. There are also wildlife habitats interspersed among the pastures and the fields and at the sides of the water-courses. Waterfowl breed unmolested in all these areas, and their numbers are swelled in winter by refugees from the bitter north of Europe. They pitch out of the turquoise and saffron sunsets of December and January to alight on shingle, grass and water, exhausted but finding rest.

There are six small towns on the Marsh. All were once busy coastal communities, and four were members of the Cinque Ports Confederation. The six towns are New Romney, Lydd, Rye, Winchelsea, Dymchurch and Hythe. The four Cinque Ports were Romney, Rye, Winchelsea and Hythe.

The origin of the Cinque Ports Confederation was probably informal. Saxon settlers on this south-east point of England realized that they would have to do something to check the increasing Viking raids or succumb. They had nothing to fear from the land, for at their backs was the vast forest of Andredsweald. But in front was the sea, and swiftly over the sea came the longships of the Vikings, brilliant sailors, skilled and pitiless warriors. The Marsh Saxons lived by both farming and fishing. They became adept at rearing beasts and building boats. They now set to work to build the kind of ships in which they could meet the Viking raiders on the high seas, and not wait to do battle on land, where they were frequently worsted. Eventually they became a match for the invaders, but it took generations to do it. Ships were built wherever it was possible to build them, and the shipyards of England's south-east corner developed a special significance by virtue of their vital strategic position looking out over the narrow seas of the Channel. They maintained their original fishing interests but also developed into naval bases.

In the eleventh century King Edward the Confessor came to an agreement with these seamen. They should provide him with ships and the men to sail them at stated periods for suitable rewards, which were generous. The King selected five Head Ports, which were Hastings, Romney, Hythe, Sandwich and Dover. These were the original Five Ports. 'Cinque' was a silly affectation not used until the sixteenth century. Until then plain English was good enough, and plain English soon dealt with the French term, the pronunciation of which was degraded to 'sink'. Rye and Winchelsea were subsequently added to the Confederation. Other ports were also bought in, each as a 'member' to one of the Head Ports. Lesser places, some not even ports, were often added as 'limbs'.

The Norman Conquest did not reduce the status of the Confederation, which had even more work to do when England and France became implacable enemies. Indeed, the Portsmen proved themselves highly proficient in the tit-for-tat raids which grew to be almost a way of life along the English south-east coast and the French north coast.

The natural capital of Romney Marsh was Romney. There are, in fact, two Romneys, New Romney and Old Romney. The two stand about a mile and a half apart, and it is uncertain how they came to be called old and new. The answer probably lies with the sea and the silt. Romney stood on an estuary where the Rother met the sea. In the thirteenth century the estuary silted up, and it is highly probable that the town expanded seaward to keep its port. The new port became New Romney. Nevertheless, its life as a port was doomed. The eleventh, twelfth and thirteenth centuries brought a series of great storms which rose to a terrifying crescendo in 1287, when a tempest savagely battered the south coast and forced the River Rother out of its course. The debris of the gale choked the mouth of the estuary, thus adding to the effect of the silt build-up, and the river found a new outlet at Rye, where it remains today despite the valiant efforts of Romney people to induce it to return.

New Romney ceased to be a port overnight, and ever since the noble church tower has looked down upon a landlocked town a mile from the sea. Once ships tied up to its wall. It is a magnificent church, built between the late eleventh century and mid-twelfth century, and its tower, in five sections with four pinnacles, can be seen for many miles across the flat and open land. You pass under the tower to reach the interior, through a rounded Norman doorway of superb proportions and zigzag decorations. You have to walk down five steps to reach the door, and all visitors wonder why such an impressive entrance was placed below the level of the road. The great tempest was responsible. It flooded the church and piled up a vast mass of debris scoured from the sea. It took a lot of manpower a long time to clear it all out, but the church was eventually restored to its former glory. Since then, however, everybody has had to step down to get in, for the floor lies at the pre-tempest land level, well below the road outside. You forget all that once you are inside. You come to a full stop the instant you pass through that door, arrested by the beauty of the strong Norman pillars and rounded arches flanking the nave.

Although the little town is now left high and dry, it still retains something of the aura of an important port and is still called the capital of the Marsh. The long High Street contains medieval and eighteenth-century buildings and impressive half-timber work. The town is unspoiled and pleasantly mellow, like a sunny September day.

Old Romney is now a scattered hamlet. Its little church stands enchantingly among flat meadows, screened by tremendous white willows, well loved and cared for. The sunlight plays upon the leaves and projects their moving shadows upon the stone walls of the church, which has stood there since the thirteenth century.

The old building lies back from a road which cuts a long line across the middle of the Marsh from New Romney to Appledore. For most of its six miles it is raised above the surrounding pastures, sometimes just a little, sometimes by several feet. That is because it follows the top of an ancient embankment called the Rhee Wall, accompanied by a channel, almost certainly the most ancient flood defence work on the Marsh. Its origin is uncertain. It is usually attributed to the Romans but it may well be older. It could have been built by the Belgae, the redoubtable Celtic tribe who inhabited large areas of the south, including parts of the Marsh, immediately before the Roman invasion. The Belgae were talented engineers. The Romans undoubtedly recognized and respected this, and might well have taken over the Rhee Wall and incorporated it in their own sea defence works. It neatly divides Romney Marsh proper on the east from Walland Marsh on the west.

The same storm which deprived New Romney of its harbour also cut off Lydd, about three miles south and a member to Romney in the Cinque Ports Confederation. You see the church tower, 132 feet high, long before you reach the town, but it is not now the solitary landmark it was once. From distant points across the level land it seems to be enshrouded in a mesh of cables and steel pylons, so you approach with trepidation. The alien industrial mess is spewed out by the Dungeness atomic power station, but when you are actually in Lydd you are mercifully almost unaware of the unlovely structures south, west and north, and you find to your great pleasure that Lydd is a very attractive place. The church stands in the centre of the town, and that superb tower soars high above trees, shallow roofs, low-hung houses, marshland and shingle. It was built in 1442-6 under the direction of a mason from Canterbury Cathedral, and it cost £280. It was joined to the western end of a long, low church built about two hundred years earlier, but it was so well done that there is no jarring note, no incongruity. The total length of the church is 199 feet. The tower is ragstone, a calcareous sandstone quarried from the lower greensand under the eastern end of the North Downs, and large numbers of churches in the Kentish part of the Weald are built of it. A Saxon building preceded the present church and there are clear traces of it in the north-west corner. The name of the place was mentioned in a Saxon eighth-century charter as Hlyda.

Nazi bombs badly damaged Lydd church in World War II. A direct hit completely destroyed the chancel and high altar in October 1940, and flying bombs added to the damage later in the war. Sensitive and skilled architectural work achieved a completely successful restoration, but first the people of Lydd had to fight a proposal to shorten the length of the church to save expense.

In the early sixteenth century Lydd had for rector a man destined for high office, fame and tragedy. He was Thomas Wolsey. Wolsey became Cardinal in 1515, and when he was immersed in affairs of state and intrigue with King Henry VIII, did he, I wonder, ever think, a little sadly perhaps, of the quiet church by the sea, calmly presiding over the market town whose charter was granted by Edward I? Wolsey died in 1530.

Small walks lead away from the circular churchyard, one to the high street, which wears the air of a thriving country town. Houses and shops cluster close together, hugging the earth in the characteristic way of nearly all the buildings of the Marsh apart from the churches. Small areas of green grass relieve the black timber, white stucco and red brick of the buildings. The strange light of the Marsh puts a kind of sheen upon the town. The inhabitants add colour in spring and summer with an abundance of flowers, often in gardens only a few yards square. There is no gradual transition from town to Marsh; the marshland reaches up to the doorsteps of the houses.

South and east lie the pebbles, pools and low scrub of Dungeness. This great triangular headland thrusts its nose south-east into the Channel towards France, less than thirty miles away. It is the biggest shingle structure in Britain and comprises a series of ridges. It is a stony wilderness, and many visitors to it are repelled by its desolation. But some are attracted by it. Naturalists go there to study its birds, its flowers and bush-like plants which spring direct from the shingle. The Royal Society for the Protection of Birds has a reserve there. Geologists go there to study its unique formation. Everybody marvels how it got there, incongruously tacked on to the edge of the grassland and cornfields.

Its creation has been long and complicated and is bound up with the strange evolution of the Marsh in general, plus the action of the sea. Wind-driven waves from both west and east piled up shingle and flints, first laying the foundations of the headland and then steadily building it up. This piling-up process is still going on, and in places the shingle is now fifty feet deep.

In the 1960s a new growth rose from the Dungarees stones, the massive atomic power station. It dominated the whole area. Thick chain-link fencing makes the place look like a concentration camp. Even worse, much worse, are the huge pylons which stride out from the station over the Marsh, linked by thick cables. Incongruous and utterly alien, they completely destroy the character of the low and level land. If ever there was a case for laying cables underground, this is it.

We now journey on to Rye and Winchelsea at the western end of the Marsh.

The two towns stand on twin hills $2\frac{1}{2}$ miles apart, divided by a wide stretch of Brede Level. They are often described as twin towns, but this is misleading, for they are entirely unlike. Both suffered badly in the great storm of 1287, but Winchelsea much more so than Rye. Winchelsea, built at sea-level, was battered to bits so thoroughly that we cannot now be sure exactly where it stood. It was completely re-built on a nearby hill and deliberately planned from start to finish. King Edward I took a close interest in its design and construction. Streets were wide and criss-crossed one another so that the town comprises a series of grids, like a Roman city. This new Winchelsea was first occupied in 1292, and the heart of the meticulously planned town was the church, at the town centre and its justifiable pride. It was designed almost to cathedral proportions and occupied an entire block in the grid system. This noble piece of architecture would have been the Cathedral of the Marsh had it not been for the ravages of the French, which, unlike those of the sea, did not abate. Attacks during the thirteenth and fourteenth centuries were frequent, savage and systematic. The French came with intent to kill, burn and destroy, and they were depressingly successful. The church was always a principal objective, partly because the great tower was also a look-out post. The final and most formidable attack came in 1449, when the French burned both Winchelsea and Rye. The church was never properly repaired after this. From the outside you seem to be looking at standing sections. Inside only the chancel and side chapels remain intact, but these in themselves comprise a huge church of great beauty.

The rebuilt Winchelsea had a wide harbour, fed by the River Brede, and for a while its maritime enterprises flourished despite the French. Then that old enemy, silt, built up and Winchelsea's life as a port ended by the end of the fifteenth century. Neglect ensued, decay followed and by the middle of the seventeenth century the town had sunk into decreptitude. When John Evelyn, the diarist, went there in 1652, he found only 'a few despicable hovels and cottages'. In 1725 Daniel Defoe found 'rather the skeleton of an ancient city than a real town', and sixty-five years later John Wesley almost repeated Defoe, referring to 'that poor skeleton of Ancient Winchelsea'.

On Brede Level the skills of the farmer replaced the skills of the mariners. Grass grew where waves had shimmered. Sheep grazed where ships had floated. That is still the picture on the Level. In the town neglect was eventually banished, and though Winchelsea has never recovered the glory, the bustle or the commercial importance, it has recovered its good looks. Today you are unlikely to find a better cared-for place anywhere. It is the darling of the tourists, who mercifully have not robbed it of its peace and quiet. Its feeling of space is emphasized by the stark battlements of Strand Gate, New Gate and Pipewell Gate, relics of the defence works built to keep out the French. But they never did.

Rye, unlike Winchelsea, was able to pick itself up and renew life after the great storm, for Rye was built upon a great sand rock which was virtually an island. The name derives from Old English, 'aet paere iege', 'at the island', which became 'atterie' and then simply 'Rie'. Rye also suffered from silting up but not on the same scale as the other Marsh ports, because Rye still had the Rother, which, with the Tillingham and the Brede, almost encircled the town and flowed on to the English Channel. Rye had one of the best harbours on the south-east coast until about the middle of the sixteenth century, when silting up became a serious problem and the town's prosperity declined. Nevertheless, Rye has never given up her seafaring traditions. She still has her quays, her Strand, her fishing fleet and some commercial craft. Modern Rÿe Harbour is little more than a harbour by name, a mile and a quarter from the town. It consists of a forlorn scattering of buildings on or round about the shingle and some tie-up facilities for small craft. But today Rye has a landward face also. It is now a busy market town and the main shopping centre for the Marsh. Also, it is paradise for thousands of tourists.

Rye has its medieval castle, the Ypres Tower, but it is not the town's most conspicuous building. That distinction goes to St Mary's parish church which stands in Church Square on the very top of the hill, from which it dominates the entire town. The houses reach up to it not on terraces but along little cobbled streets which climb steeply to the summit from sea-level. You see its massive tower from points far out on the Marsh, you see it from the sea and from Winchelsea across Brede Level, and it is the first building to catch your eye as you approach from the landward side. It was built between 1150 and 1300, but the French destroyed it in 1377, when they burnt practically the whole town to the ground. It was rebuilt during the fifteenth century, and the builders were able to incorporate some remnants of the older building which are easily picked out. The best-known feature of the church is the clock on the north side of the tower. Cherubs strike bells at the quarter hours but not on the hour.

The Ypres Tower is nothing to do with the Ypres in Flanders, still a household word throughout the world because of the tragic slaughter there in the First World War. It stands squat, square and grim, with a round tower at each corner, on the edge of a former clifftop, where it was built about 1250 as a principal part of the town's defences against the French. It was sold to a private buyer in 1430, when money was still badly needed to repair the ravages of the 1377 raid. His name was John de Ypres.

You soon forget the hazards of the cobbled streets in the sheer enchantment of your surroundings. It is hard to believe that there could be so much harmony in such a medley of bricks, tiles, stones and ancient timber. The most famous of the houses is the Mermaid Inn, dating mostly from the fifteenth century but partly older.

The two other coastal towns, Dymchurch and Hythe, are both east of New Romney. Dymchurch is now a small seaside resort and huddles under the sea wall. Much new building in the area threatens to smother the old town, from which for many centuries the Marsh was administered by gentlemen called the Lords of Romney Marsh. They sat for the last time as an administrative court in 1951.

Hythe, at the very edge of the Marsh, is also now a seaside resort. Evidence of the former prosperous Cinque Port is scant, but once an ample harbour offered safe anchorage for both merchant and naval vessels. The port became choked in the reign of Queen Elizabeth I. Today the town climbs landward to a magnificent church on the higher ground, the product of medieval seafaring prosperity. A modern extension of the town on the coast is the answer to families with children who want a reasonably quiet seaside holiday but like an occasional excursion into sophistication. Folkestone, about four miles away, is ready to greet them. So is the miniature Romney, Hythe and Dymchurch Railway, which runs fourteen miles from Hythe to Dungeness.

The villages of the central Marsh are little more than hamlets, with one exception, Brookland, once called Brook. The best way to

get to Brookland, though not the easiest, is to set out from Lydd
north-west along narrow lanes. From these byways you see miles
of the Marsh at its most interesting, and you also feel its silence
and loneliness. I remember with pleasure an evening in early
autumn when I took one of those lanes, having decided to drive to
Appledore by way of Brookland. Distant tree-covered hills rose far
to my west, but the Marsh stretched vastly away to the east, empty
but for the sheep. In four miles I met no car and only three riders,
and the track was so narrow I had to stop to let them pass in single
file, smiling their 'thank-you' as they rode by.

Brookland stands in the middle of the Marsh, a compact street, a
farm, a few houses on the outskirts, and a church. Tremendous
willows and ash trees shelter it, and on the level expanses you
should be able to see it for miles. But you can't, and you are
practically in the village before you realize it. How is it that so
many marsh villages are invisible until you are almost there?

When I first went to Brookland, I rubbed my eyes in
astonishment for in the churchyard beside the porch somebody
had pitched a huge wigwam. It was, of course, nothing of the kind.
It was a detached belfry built like a steeple, and everybody
assumes either that it was intended to place it on the church tower
or that once it actually did rest on the tower and was taken down
for some reason not yet discovered. The most likely explanation,
however, is that an open-air belfry was built at the same time as
the church, about 1260, that in due course a shelter was added to
protect bells and ringers and that eventually the protective
cladding was extended to cover the entire structure. There are three
sections to the belfry, which is sixty feet high and now clad with
shingles. On the top a wrought-iron weather vane swings in the
air. It is supposed to be a winged dragon. It looks more like a wild
duck in flight with an unfortunate development to its tail, which is
long, wriggly and spiked. Bells are still rung from this strange
belfry. The circular lead font in the church is probably the best of
the few leaden fonts in Britain. It bears workmanship which may
have been carried out by twelfth-century Norman or Flemish
craftsmen.

The Marsh might have been specially made for smugglers, for
France is so near, about thirty miles off, and goods could be
transported swiftly to safety along devious paths and tracks across

bogs and through thick and extensive beds of reed. The most conscientious and intrepid body of Excise men would have been reckless in the extreme to follow suspects into those reeds beds. Failure would have been certain, injury probable, death more than possible. Brookland was an important transit point on a carefully organized route to London, and the church was probably one of many safe hiding-places for merchandise brought up from Lydd, whose inhabitants were deep in the 'free-trade' business. Every man's hand seemed against the Excise, from parsons to sheep-lookers on the Marsh, who were invaluable guides.

But law and order sometimes got their way. One night in February 1821, a smuggling party comprising not only carriers but also a fifty-strong armed escort set out to receive an important consignment. It was a carefully disciplined body. But the party was surprised by the Coast Blockade established five years earlier. Shots were exchanged. The smugglers were well trained and they successfully unloaded the cargo from the boats under the protective fire of their escort. But then came the trickiest part. They had to retreat into the Marsh to a place of refuge. They couldn't do it. The Blockade stuck too close. A fierce battle developed. In this the Blockade's officer and four smugglers were wounded. The ensuing trial at the Old Bailey aroused national interest, and the Battle of Brookland was re-fought in more peaceful gatherings in inns and by kitchen firesides all over the country for a very long time.

As at Lydd, the Marsh pastures reach up to the doorsteps of Brookland, so that you are quickly back on the small roads, in the big spaces and the silence. Suddenly you are aware of a modest church with a modest spire far out among the pastures, alone on a patch of raised ground with waterways all round and not another building in sight. It is a modern church with ancient origins, possibly Norman. It fell into disrepair and was rebuilt in 1913. A wayside notice tells you it is the church of St Thomas à Becket, Fairfield. But where is or where was Fairfield? Today it is the name of a district, and the church serves the people who live in isolated houses and farms. Here is the essence of the Marsh, its very heart. The wind makes a soft sound in the grass, you hear the sheep cropping the pastures, and in the distance a redshank's sharp, warning cry which rises, then falls away, on a long descending note into the stillness.

The lane comes to an abrupt stop on the banks of a wide stretch of water which you will naturally believe to be a river. It is, in fact, the Royal Military Canal, cut at the beginning of the nineteenth century as a defence against an anticipated Napoleonic invasion. It makes a semi-circle for twenty-three miles below the prehistoric cliffs from Hythe to a point just north of Rye, where it joins the River Rother. No invading force ever reached this water barrier, which is now a quiet retreat enjoyed alike by residents, visitors and waterfowl.

The sturdy tower of Appledore church the other side of the canal rises above the treetops. A bridge takes you over, and on the instant you are transported from the hair-breadth width of the lanes to sudden spaciousness, for Appledore, on the western rim of the Marsh, is a big, roomy and handsome village, and if there were a beauty contest for Marsh villages Appledore would probably win it. *The Anglo-Saxon Chronicle* refers to it as 'Apuldre', 'apple tree', and this pure Saxon word was still in common use by country people forty years ago. When I was a boy I frequently heard in conversation the phrase 'that ole apple dree'. The broad main street is flanked by houses of many ages and many architectural styles, but the village was not always as quiet as it is today. *The Anglo-Saxon Chronicle* describes a big Danish invasion in 892, when a powerful force, carried by 250 ships up the Rother, captured the village and established a base from which they began an invasion of England. They pillaged their way north as far as Cheshire but were eventually checked by King Alfred the Great. The church is largely a reconstruction of an earlier building burnt by the French raiders in 1380.

A road offers swift and easy passage from Appledore to Tenterden, but we shall not take it for we are not yet ready to leave the Marsh. First there is the Isle of Oxney (oxen island) about two miles south-west. The Marsh surrounds it, but it still feels like the island it once was, rising from sea-level to about two hundred feet. The island supports a scattered village, Stone, and a surprisingly large church built in 1484 after a fire had demolished an earlier building. Great ash trees surround it, with a mingling of horse-chestnut trees and oaks; and from the churchyard there are magnificent views across the Rother Levels. Oxney is about six miles long and three miles deep, and the steep fall of the land in places invokes a sense of antique cliffs.

A relic in the church vividly catches the imagination in a different way. At first it seems no more than the battered remains of a stone column. It is, in fact, a third-century ragstone Roman altar used in the worship of Mithras. On its side, carved in relief, you can just trace the outline of a sacrificial bull, and the top is shaped into a circular declivity, perhaps for sacrificial ceremony. The altar has stood in the church since 1926, when it was rescued from the pull-up of a nearby inn, where it did humiliating duty as a mounting block for riders. Perhaps it came from Roman Lemanis, just off the Marsh twelve miles east.

Wittersham, on the western edge of Oxney, is a pleasant medley of old and new with a church of noble proportions built of ragstone and sandstone, mostly in the fourteenth century. A beacon on top of the tall tower brought ships safely up the Rother in the Middle Ages. They tied up at a place called Smallhythe, which was the port, just off the island, for Tenterden had nothing to do with Hythe at the eastern end of the Marsh. It was a thriving maritime and shipbuilding town and at one time comprised more houses than Tenterden. A hamlet among trees bordered by a straight stretch of water, the Reading sewer, is what remains of the busy port. There are many such 'sewers' on the Marsh, but they are not the kind so vital to urban life. They are stretches of clear water drained from the land and connected with waterways to the sea.

In Smallhythe you are brought face to face with everybody's dream house. It is closely timbered in black oak with muted, creamy fill-in, and the top storey liberally overhangs the ground floor but not enough to keep the sun off. There are small red tiles on the roof with a tall chimney at each end, and a barn and low outbuildings are grouped round about, roofed with the same small tiles. This admixture of black, red and cream is set off by the green of informal lawns. The lovely house was built in 1480 and was the headquarters of the Smallhythe port officer. Fire badly damaged it in 1516, but it was rebuilt with care and taste. The name of the house is Smallhythe Place, and it was the actress Ellen Terry's home from 1899, when she bought it, until her death in 1928. The National Trust owns it now and has made of it a memorial museum in honour of her. A contemporary and rather similar house, the Priest's House, stands nearby, and visitors often mistake it for Ellen Terry's home.

At this point we take our leave of the Marsh.

3

The Garden of England

From Ellen Terry's house the lane develops a firm upward trend, out of the Marsh. Trees immediately become a more integral part of the landscape, no longer individually as on the Marsh, where a single free-standing willow or ash can be a landmark for miles, but as groups and belts. You now see the woods first and the trees second. The lane climbs steadily for about two miles and then levels out to set you down abruptly in Tenterden's broad and beautiful High Street. Here you stand on the doorstep of the Garden of the England.

Tenterden is a busy little town but it is not marred by the frenzy which is now such a sorry feature of so many of our towns. There is a feeling of unhasty efficiency about it. There is plenty of elbow room, and there is grace as well as space. Shops and houses stand cheek by jowl on both sides of the street, whose generous proportions, however, dispel any sense of constriction. The variety of architecture is astonishing, and that applies to age as well as style and size. Close-set black oak in timber-framed houses contrasts with white plaster. Some of these houses were built in the fifteenth century, and often you find a building with an eighteenth- or nineteenth-century front but heavily beamed interiors which indicate a much older origin. The Woolpack Inn and the Eight Bells Inn, facing each other across the street, are excellent examples. And there are weatherboarded houses, usually white but sometimes black; houses with walls of hanging tiles, handsome buildings from the eighteenth century, including the town hall built in 1790 to replace an older building destroyed by fire in 1661. Some roofs are higher than others. Some have steeper inclines. Some have wavy ridges, some are dead straight. But nothing jars. Nothing looks incongruous.

Little lanes wriggle away from the High Street, momentarily pushing aside the houses, and from these inconspicuous ways

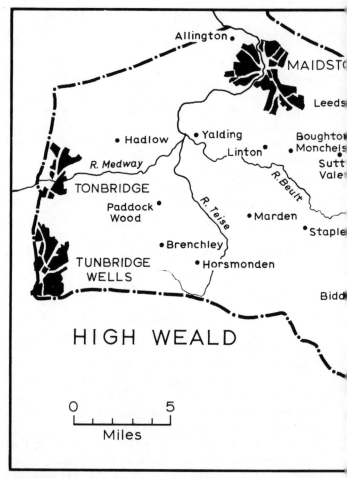

The Garden of England

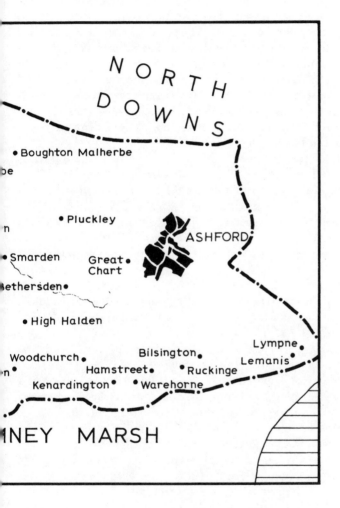

N O R T H
D O W N S

• Boughton Malherbe

be

n

• Pluckley

• Smarden

Great •
Chart

ASHFORD

ethersden •

• High Halden

Woodchurch •

Bilsington •

Lympne •

Lemanis •

n •

Hamstreet •

• Ruckinge

Kenardington •

• Warehorne

NEY   MARSH

there are enchanting views of the 'backs', glimpses of an older, homely town, though not of Tenterden's origin. That was some centuries earlier and is not architectural. Towards the end of the seventh century land where the town now stands was granted to Minster Abbey and convent in Thanet. Pigs were reared on this land, a clearing in the forest; at the end of summer they were killed and salted, and in that state of preservation were transported about forty miles to Thanet to provide the abbess and her nuns with food through the winter. And that was how Tenterden got its name. It became known as 'Tentwardene', which, says *The Oxford Dictionary of English Place Names*, means 'the denn or swine pasture of the Thanet people'.

By far the most prominent piece of architecture in the town is the tower of the parish church. It soars above the buildings clustered round it, and it dominates the countryside. It is 120 feet high and stands on ground 200 feet above sea-level. It is a landmark easily recognized from far out in the Weald, and from the top on a clear day you can see the coast of France. It was built in 1461-3 of Bethersden 'marble', and there is a tall pinnacle at each corner. Construction of the church began in the twelfth century, almost certainly on the site of an earlier building, and it has grown through the centuries. It is dedicated to St Mildred, grand-daughter of King Egbert, and second Abbess of Minster. She died about 720. It is a pity the interior is so dim, for a fine barrel ceiling, probably of the fifteenth century, panelled and beautifully carved, is lost in the shadows.

Tenterden was admitted to the Cinque Ports Confederation as a Limb of Rye in 1450, with ships based at Smallhythe. King Henry VIII visited Tenterden in 1537, and twelve years later his ship the *Grand Masters* was rebuilt in the Smallhythe shipyards. The 400-ton vessel was designed to carry 250 armed men.

Tenterden was an important exporter of wool during the medieval sheep boom, but in the fourteenth century emphasis was switched from exports to home manufacturers. To inject new life into a lagging cloth trade, King Edward III invited Flemish weavers to Kent in 1331. They were asked to impart their skills to the Kentish craftsmen. They succeeded. The resident weavers took to the new skills avidly. Tenterden, with an abundance of wool on the Marsh, became a thriving centre of the weaving industry, and its broadcloth rose rapidly in popularity. Similar enterprises sprang up in the Wealden villages. Like Tenterden, they concentrated on broadcloth, which they produced in varied colours. The wool regulations were revised, and exports of wool were now banned. A new law protected the weavers by prohibiting both the export of English wool and the import of overseas cloth. Kentish broadcloth sold readily not only at home but also on the Continent, competing easily with the Continental products. The cloth-manufacturers grew rich, and you can often hear an echo of the industry in the Kentish surname Weaver.

It is tempting to strike due north at once from Tenterden, straight into the ancient county of Kent, turning your back on the Marsh once and for all. To do so would be to miss a fascinating narrow belt of countryside which is not Marsh and yet is not entirely divorced from the Marsh. So you go east and along the crest of the ancient cliffs which enclosed the prehistoric bay. You follow the B2067 but take great care not to stray to B2080, which is all too easy and will take you back to Appledore. Views open up almost at once, over the level pastures, over the Royal Military Canal and innumerable little waterways gleaming in the grass, with the glittering expanses of the sea beyond. The farther east you go, the more extensive the views become.

Villages are scattered along this antique ridge. The first is Woodchurch, a large village, but you could easily pass it, for it contrives to hide itself along a by-road going north. The church captures your attention immediately. It has a short, sturdy tower and a tall, shingled spire. It is a striking exterior but the interior is outstandingly beautiful, stone and timber complementing each other, clean and uncluttered, poetry in architecture.

Kenardington might also go unnoticed because, again, the village stands on a by-road, this time to the south towards the Marsh. What strikes your eye long before you reach the village is what seems obviously a massive fort on a hilltop above the flats. Actually, it is the church, or, more accurately, part of the church. Lightning struck the thirteenth-century building in 1559, and damage to the nave and chancel was not repaired. What was the south aisle is now the whole church. The view over the Marsh from the churchyard is panoramic. Pine trees add a touch of drama.

The villages follow one another in well-spaced succession, Warehorne, Ham Street, Ruckinge, Bilsington, always with the expanse of the Marsh on your right. Do not hurry. The villages may not have much to offer the guidebooks or the tourists intent on seeing what they think they ought to see. They are just lovely in a quiet and unspectacular way, and that, in a brash and frenetic world, is something to treasure. Sometimes the road sinks almost to marsh-level, but mostly you are well above the flat pastures, on the edge of the ancient cliffs. Woods press upon you on the landward side, hazel, hawthorn and alder brushing the surface of the narrow road. Eventually the land becomes imbued with fixed purpose and lifts steadily, sweeping away in long curves, until at last you come to Lympne, pronounced 'Limm', and up there, 350 feet above the sea, you see all that vast grass-bound bay spread out below you like a map.

At Lympne, the Roman Lemanis, you follow in the steps of the legionaries, for this was almost certainly one of the three key points in the great invasion of AD 43. The other two probabilities are Richborough and Dover. Evidence suggests that the Romans built a harbour at Lemanis, and towards the end of the third century they built a formidable ten-acre fortress, one of a string of fortresses guarding the 'Saxon Shore'. Little is left of this impressive military structure: a few remnants of the wall, lumps of masonry scattered about among the grasses, where from the distance they look like sleeping sheep. That is all. These remains, meagre though they are, bear a resounding name, Stutfall Castle. There is nothing Latin about this word. It is clearly Saxon, and there is a suggestion that it may mean 'stout wall'. But the Saxons came as farmers, though also trained to warfare, and *The Origin of English Place Names* suggests 'stod-fald', an enclosure for a stud of horses. The Saxons often used such old enclosures for horse-folds.

About a thousand years after the Romans built Stutfall Castle, another castle was built just above the Roman fortress, at the highest point of the old cliffs, but on nothing like the same scale. This is Lympne Castle, more a roomy manor house with moderate defences than a castle. Through the centuries it was altered, underwent modifications and achieved additions. Then it fell on bad times and it was in a sorry state at the beginning of this century, when it was given a thorough restoration by Sir Robert Lorimer. The earliest part is contained in a square tower at the east end. The view from Lympne Castle across the Marsh is magnificent.

The nearby church looks at first glance just as much like a fort as the castle does, if not more. This is due to the powerful appearance of the Norman tower, which rises from the centre of the building. It was built 1100-1110. The rest of the church was originally of the same time, and, like its neighbour, it has been added to, altered and enlarged as generations have passed.

At the northern end of Lympne village we are back with the Romans, for here the B2068 invites you inland, running in the characteristic Roman dead straight line across the North Downs and on to Durovernum, which we call Canterbury, and so out of the Weald. The Saxons called it Stane Street. They did not know what the Romans called it, and neither do we, and we must not be tempted out of our territory.

We turn our attention to Ashford, but before taking a final farewell of Lympne, let us reflect a moment on the name. It is not a derivative of Lemanis. It is an older, Celtic word for a branch of the Rother which flowed into the sea about where Hythe stands now. The settlement took its name from the river.

Ashford lies in a great gap of the North Downs, north-west of Lympne. The simplest way to get there is up the A20, about eight miles, but personally I would leave that traffic-cursed road to the rushing motorist anxious to reach Folkestone and the sea. It is infinitely more pleasant to drive along unclassified lanes through pastoral and wooded countryside. It takes longer, but what of that? It is a withdrawn countryside, sometimes rather nondescript, broken by small farms with small meadows populated by a few cattle, and here and there a horse or two. Industrial installations indicate that you are nearing the town, but beyond, your eyes lift to the clean, redeeming lines of the Downs.

Ashford is an industrial town, and first impressions of it are apt to be depressing. Yet it is not dirty. It is not even grubby. You feel that somehow it has lost its way. It has been an important market town since the thirteenth century, and its present weekly cattle market is still one of the biggest and one of the most important in the country. The town became an industrial centre in the middle of the nineteenth century with the coming of the railways. Ashford, already the junction of five major roads, became also the junction of four railway lines with extensive locomotive workshops. The workshops created a factory town, rows of red Victorian houses, superimposed on the old town which owed its existence to the agriculture and the rural industries of the surrounding countryside. Modern development has also in places had a jarring effect. Functional structures devoid of character are thrust hard up against mellow timber-framed buildings which look as if they are about to be elbowed out of the way.

But the heart of the town is lovely: a little square and a big ragstone church with a central tower 120 feet high and an interior like a cathedral. Building began in the fourteenth century and the church quickly grew. Seventeenth- and eighteenth-century houses look inward over the square to the church, whose tower, of course, is the dominating feature. Narrow streets take you out of the square, and here, too, you find small and graceful houses of the sixteenth and seventeenth centuries.

We now turn due west, back towards Tenterden, along either the A28 or the quiet by-roads. Villages are plentiful in this part of the Kentish Weald, and their names have a resounding Saxon ring. Footpaths are also plentiful, linking village to village and road to road; a good map is essential.

You reach the first of these villages, Great Chart, when you are scarcely out of Ashford. It was a much bigger village when the Saxons lived there, but the Danes, coming up from Appledore, burnt it to the ground in 893. It is graced by a ragstone church of the thirteenth-fourteenth century and there are some medieval buildings.

About four miles on you arrive at Bethersden, where you need to linger long. Here are memories of a man in whose life the strands of love, military service and poetry ran equally strong. At Bethersden you are in the land of the Lovelaces; and the lyrics of Richard Lovelace, handsome, talented and devoted Cavalier, stand high in the ranks of English literature. His farewell to Lucasta, on 'going to the warres', is famous:

I could not love thee, Deare, so much,
    Loved I not Honour more.

And when, in 1642, he was imprisoned for demanding that the King should be restored to his rights, he continued his defiance of the Puritans in words now equally famous:

Stone walls do not a prison make,
  Nor iron bars a cage;
Minds innocent and quiet take
  That for a hermitage.
If I have freedom in my love,
  And in my soul am free,
Angels alone that soar above
  Enjoy such liberty.

More people are familiar with the first two lines of that passage than with the name of the poet who wrote them. Lovelace's courage and loyalty cost him his entire fortune, and he died in 1658 in desperate want, when he was only forty. There is a Lovelace Chapel in Bethersden church, and a portrait of the poet by an unknown painter hangs in Dulwich College picture gallery.

The church, on its knoll, is an arresting building, mostly of ragstone, and its tower easily overtops the surrounding trees, an important look-out post in the days when invasion threatened from the French or Spanish. It was brought back to similar service in this century when the threat came from the Nazis.

When you go into a building, you seldom glance at the floor you walk on, but you should pause to do so when you pass through the porch of Bethersden church, for it is paved with fine slabs of 'marble' quarried in the district. There is more of it in other parts of the church, more elsewhere in this eastern, Kentish Weald, and a great deal of similar 'marble' in the Weald of Sussex. When shown examples of it, visitors are inclined to polite disbelief, often suspecting some kind of joke, but their doubts are unfounded. There actually is such marble, as we have already noted, though it is not the marble of Michelangelo. It is a form of limestone produced by the massed fossilized shells of the freshwater snail called *Viviparus Paludina.* It takes on a pleasing greenish-grey lustre when polished. Not only church floors were made of it, but also fonts, and, as we have seen, Tenterden church tower was built of it. It was also used in houses, often for fireplaces. The 'marble' was quarried, until the end of the last century, from the Wealden clay through which it ran in seams about a foot thick and usually twenty to thirty feet below the surface. I have always marvelled that out of the unkind clay should come this exquisite material, lined and shot with subtle colours. When you stroke the smooth surface, your fingers scan millions of years.

In the churchyard you cannot fail to notice a strange flattened mound with sealed 'doors' facing a path. The mound contains tombs of a local type irreverently called 'oven vaults'. They were constructed in 1796 for three families, the Jacksons, Wilmots and Witherdens.

In little more than three miles you are in High Halden, for which the Saxons had a name rivalling anything the Welsh can do, Habinwoldungdene, which possibly meant, suggests *The Oxford Dictionary of English Place Names*, 'the denne of Habuweald's people'.

The outstanding feature of High Halden is its parish church, which, says Sheila Kaye-Smith in *The Weald of Kent and Sussex*, 'must contain more timber than any other church in the Weald'. Its belfry tower and spire, visible for miles around, are constructed entirely of timber. Tower, spire and west entrance are said to have taken about fifty tons of oak. Massive timber work also distinguishes the interior of the church itself.

We have now travelled a sort of oval and we are back within a short distance of Tenterden, on the north side of the town. It is to the north that we now direct our steps.

The first thing you notice is the similarity of the countryside to Romney Marsh. You almost feel the Marsh is going with you. Here are the same well-cared-for pastures, the same great willows, the same Romney sheep, the quick flashes of water. But soon the nature of the countryside begins to change, subtly at first and then very definitely. Pasture ceases to be the predominant feature, and you enter a land of intensive cultivation, a land of orchards and hop gardens, of vegetables and horticultural nurseries, interspersed with small meadows and fields of corn. The cultivations reach to the very edges of the roadsides, but here and there you find yourself travelling between tall hedges, much taller than a man is high. These are the traditional windbreaks and shelters for the orchards, and once they were far more numerous than they are today. The modern grower maintains the high hedgerows where strong and cold winds are general but elsewhere he prefers the free movement of air which, with the sunshine, encourages maximum cropping from the trees.

It is a busy countryside. Nowhere else in the kingdom is land more scientifically or more intensively tilled, and nowhere else is land induced so consistently, year after year, to yield to the very utmost of its capacity. Big fruit crops are backed up by scientifically constructed stores, so that gluts are avoided in the autumn and you and I can go on eating quality English apples and pears until May. This productive countryside is the true Garden of England. The term has been made to cover practically all Kent, but here, you feel, it is particularly merited.

It is not tourist country, yet visitors arrive by carloads and coachloads every spring, when the landscape bursts into a glory of blossom. Special 'blossom trails' are signposted. The cherry orchards are the loveliest. Trusses of pure white flowers entirely cover the trees so that they look like earth-bound clouds. Against a background of blue sky, the flowering cherry has no equal. But the cherry orchards are far fewer than they were. They have given way to apples and pears, particularly apples, whose pink and white blossom immediately follows the cherries. But there has been a horticultural revolution here. Once, like the cherries, the apples were borne on big standard trees which you could walk under. Now the apple orchards are comprised almost entirely of bush trees, which yield higher crops and are much easier to pick. Apple-picking time is the one other period of the year which draws visitors, but this time they come specially to take on the paid job of picking, which they often combine with a holiday. Many pickers are students and other young people.

Growers are very anxious people at blossom time. These few weeks are the most crucial period in their entire year. One night's freak frost, one hour's vicious blow from the north-east accompanied by hail, can reduce the most promising crop to blackened ruin. The growers live at a high peak of tension until the blossom no longer hangs on the boughs but lies evenly on the ground, where it looks almost as lovely as it did on the trees. From then on the talk in the little inns will be about the quality of the 'set', which means the little embryo fruit left by the fallen blossom, the 'petal drop'. After that the great hope is for warm sun.

Then there are the hops. Hop-picking was once done exclusively by families from the East End of London, and the same families would go year by year to the same hop gardens. Today machines do it, and electric power dries the hops, thereby rendering redundant the traditional hop kilns. But the characteristics cones of the kilns remain as familiar a part of the Kentish landscape as they always have. The oasthouses have been converted into either farm store buildings or human habitations. Many of these residential conversions are delightful.

There is no straightforward route by which you can explore the area, which is an intricate pattern of lanes, villages and farm land. You need to go this way and that and frequently double back on yourself. By such unhasty means you will come first to apprehend the spirit of the work-a-day world you travel through, and then to enjoy it. A considerable aid to your enjoyment is the number of inns where you get a warm welcome and a pleasant meal at a reasonable price.

The villages are old and attractive and fit so snugly into the landscape that they seem to have grown there, which in a sense they have, for they are built of materials taken from the earth nearby. Each is a centre for the vital industry of food production that surrounds them, the only industry in the world which is self-renewing, taking nourishment from the earth but also, through careful husbandry, putting nourishment back.

Biddenden is the best known of these villages. It has a short, wide and remarkable street, paved on both sides with slabs of Bethersden marble, not smooth and polished but rough hewn. On one side rise buildings in architectural styles ranging from Tudor onwards, while on the other side one long, wavy, steep and tiled roof surmounts a variety of half-timbered shops and dwellings. Just beyond the street there is a long, half-timbered, seven-gabled building called the Old Cloth Hall, built in the sixteenth and seventeenth centuries. Here the word 'hall' does not mean a house. It was a place where weavers made their cloth. We should call it a factory.

You look straight down this street to the church, which stands just the right distance apart so that church and village exactly balance each other. Without the one the other would be lacking.

This view from the street also gives the church perspective, so that you can the better appreciate the bold, curiously slim, battlemented tower with the turret in one corner, which is such a characteristic of this region. It is built of Bethersden marble cut in small blocks. The rest of the church is mostly sandstone, and it has changed little since the thirteenth and fourteenth centuries.

But Biddenden is chiefly renowned not because of its long perspectives, its ancient church or its history but because of a biological curiosity, its Siamese twins, Eliza and Mary Chulkhurst. The world knows them as the Biddenden Maids. They were born probably about the middle of the sixteenth century, joined at the shoulders and hips. In that state they lived for thirty-four years, not in seclusion but taking part in the life of the community. When one died, the other would not be severed and within six hours followed her sister into death. But not into oblivion. The story of the Biddenden Maids remains very much alive and is commemorated on the village sign, where they are drawn in Elizabethan costume. They bequeathed land to the Biddenden churchwardens and their successors, stipulating that from the income bread and cheese should be given annually to the poor of the parish. The land became known as the bread and cheese lands.

Smarden, about three miles north-east of Biddenden, justifies a special journey and a lot of time spent in it. Times without number I have heard Smarden called the perfect village. One is apt to pay little attention to such high praise in these days of much vaunting and over-rating in order to bolster up the mediocre and even, sometimes, the unworthy, for the sake of tourism. But once you have been to Smarden, you cannot but agree. In more tourist-conscious districts Smarden would be host to coachloads of visitors. There would be Smarden souvenirs, antique shops and ye olde tea-rooms. But Smarden does not seek to project its image. It is content to be itself, a working place among the orchards and the fields. Yet, strolling about the village, you sense that here is something subtly different, and this sense does not deceive you. Smarden was a market town with a charter granted by King Edward III in 1332 and another, confirming Edward's, by Queen Elizabeth I in 1576. A copy of Elizabeth's charter hangs in the nave of the church. Smarden did not expand as Tenterden did, but you feel something of the dignity and the commercial influence of a medieval town as you walk among its venerable buildings.

Your first and lasting impression is of black-and-white timber-framed houses and houses of white weatherboards, all scrupulously clean, with abundant flowers and trees. There is one compact street, and there are also cottages standing alone and cottages in groups. You always end up in a tiny square, from which you emerge by passing under part of a weatherboarded house, to find yourself gazing up at the massive, battlemented church tower with a turret in the north-east corner. This church is both beautiful and big, even by Kentish standards. Its size, its wealth of timber and its freedom from clutter have earned it the affectionate title 'the barn of Kent'. It was built of Bethersden marble, rubble and some ragstone in the fourteenth and fifteenth centuries.

There are many echoes of the cloth trade which gave Smarden its prosperity, for instance the heavily timbered sixteenth-century Cloth Hall, the fourteenth-century Dragon House built by the Flemish family Pell, and the early sixteenth-century Thatched House, all weavers' dwellings. You cannot walk far in Smarden without coming face to face with architectural beauty, usually modest in size, simple in style but gracious and lovely to look at.

Pluckley, about $3\frac{1}{2}$ miles up the road, is entirely different. For a moment you feel you may have trespassed into the precincts of a religious order, owing to the long double-arched and lance-shaped windows of the cottages. They were installed by Sir Edward Cholmeley Dering in the nineteenth century. He did it to all the buildings on his Surrenden Dering estate. He thought the windows were lucky. The ragstone church overlooking the cottages grew from the thirteenth century to the seventeenth. At nearby Little Chart you will find the same 'lucky' windows, an ironic term here because the Nazi bombs of the 1939-45 war damaged the medieval church beyond repair.

You now draw close to the North Downs, running sharply south-east to Folkestone and Dover. But look westward and you see a level plain stretching far away. This area is probably the most intensively cultivated of all. Villages, fields, orchards, hop gardens, meadows and belts of woodland are welded together in close-knit harmony.

It is a curious experience crossing this flat, munificent land. The wild has no place here. It has been utterly banished. No wet, untidy corner calls to mind the jungle of Andredsweald. All has been subjugated to the service of man, and travelling through the man-made landscape you are keenly aware that you are a visitor, though not an intruder. On the contrary you sense a welcome and a homeliness, largely due to the moderate scale of things. Orchards and hop gardens come in varied shapes and sizes, sheep and cattle graze pastures which also vary in size and shape, roomy farmhouses sit comfortably among the fruit trees. Some are centuries old and heavily timbered. It is a neat and compact countryside. A little to the north there is a long, conspicuous ridge which most visitors after a cursory glance at the map mistakenly believe to be part of the North Downs. It is, in fact, part of the sandstone belt which, as we have already noted, follows the entire ranges of both North and South Downs.

A string of villages reaches across the plain. The branches of the apple and cherry trees all but brush the windows and the eaves of the cottages, whose gardens and roofs are covered with white and pink petals in spring. Headcorn, which was a busy centre for the weaving industry, has an ample high street graced by two cloth halls, an arresting war memorial and a fourteenth/fifteenth-century church, very much an integral part of the village.

Westward you come to the cottages of Staplehurst, overlooking the flat land and presided over by a characteristically large church, with a magnificent fourteenth-century timbered aisle roof and a mystery door in the south wall. Unknown craftsmen made this door about 1050 to fit the present pointed arch. Craftsmen forged for it legendary creatures in iron. They probably once covered the entire face of the door, but today they are gathered together on the top half. The church you see was started about 1200 but probably succeeded a Saxon church. The ironwork on the door tells the story of Ragnarok, the Norse Day of Judgement. Experts think it unlikely that this highly skilled smithing was done for an earlier Saxon church, so, as it could not have been done for the church we see, where did it come from? The problem is posed in a very readable guide to the church, which also explains Ragnarok, in which nature is thrown into chaos, as the ironwork shows.

Marden, still westward, is a household word among growers both in the Kent Weald and far beyond, because every year it stages a fruit show at which growers from far and wide exhibit the best of their produce. Marden was once a place of consequence. From the establishment of the Norman administration until the seventeenth century it had its own court with authority over the county sheriff. The Court House, weatherboarded, is still there.

At Horsmonden you come to a concentration of hop gardens but with no diminishing of orchards. The reverse, if anything, for Horsmonden is not only a big fruit area but also an important apple-distribution centre for markets.

In two more miles you are at Brenchley, which is a choice focal point on the blossom trail, not because there is more bloom here than elsewhere but because at Brenchley the land lifts from the plain in a series of quiet curves, and on a clear day you gaze at pink and white arcs rising to the blue sky. The coaches pass slowly here and usually stop at a few pre-selected viewpoints. From one of these you are presented with a memorable picture, the sandstone church tower standing up from the massed blossom, which flows onward and upward to the skyline above the tower's turreted top. An avenue of dark and ancient yews leading to the church door is a strong contrast to the bright blossom.

In Brenchley itself the blossom meets a rival. It is the most outstanding feature in the village and captures your entire interest. It is called the Old Palace because it was once a palace maintained for the archbishops of Canterbury. It has a liberal overhang with a spectacular use of black, perpendicular timbers. It was built in the fifteenth century but has been much restored. The impressive front itself, which catches your immediate attention, is not original but a skilled restoration.

Paddock Wood, two miles due south, is altogether different from any of the villages we have so far visited. It is new. It is also somewhat brash, but it is not without taste. It is a good shopping centre, and a very good public library occupies a place of honour in the main street. Industrial and commercial enterprises have made their homes there, including the headquarters of the Hops Marketing Board, the first of the agricultural boards. Bombs destroyed the church in 1940, and a new one built of red brick in 1953 is influenced neither by the ecclesiastical architecture of the past nor by the hard, inhuman, mathematical lines of so much architecture today. Personally, I find it graceful and dignified, a place where you might well open your mind to 'the still, small voice'.

Reading sewer, Smallhythe. On Romney Marsh 'sewer' means a channel cut to drain the land

Fairfield church, one of the loneliest spots on Romney Marsh

Detached belfry in Brookland churchyard

Ellen Terry's home, Smallhythe Place

Fourteenth-century College of Priests, Maidstone

Still northward, Hadlow has a Saxon church enlarged by the Normans, an extraordinary folly tower, and the nationally important Hadlow College of Agriculture and Horticulture.

Hadlow almost touches the fringe of Tonbridge, which in many minds is linked with Tunbridge Wells, and justifiably so, for Tunbridge Wells takes its name from Tonbridge, much the older town. Tonbridge was the nearest town to the 'healing' waters discovered in 1609, and these accordingly became known as the 'Tonbridge wells'. When a new town grew up around the waters it was, naturally, called Tonbridge or Tunbridge Wells. The spelling fluctuated freely until 1844 and the coming of the railway, when 'Tunbridge Wells' with a 'u' was firmly established. The story of this town is told in the next chapter.

Meanwhile, we can stroll by the slowly flowing River Medway at Tonbridge, with a lengthy pause at the remains of a castle overlooking the placid water. The Saxons built a fortress there, the Normans replaced it with their own castle, which was strengthened from time to time. The most impressive addition was a great gatehouse erected in the thirteenth century. Cromwell slighted (dismantled) the castle in 1646.

We have now reached the edge of the plain and find the countryside influenced by two major factors in addition to the orchards and the hop gardens, which are as thick as ever. These are Maidstone and the Medway. Here the sandstone ridge splits, and the North Downs, which have been completely blocked, are now clear and close. Between the ridge and the Downs lies a deep and narrow valley, west to east. Through the gap the River Medway flows northward with considerable purpose, changing to an eastward course along the valley. About four miles up the valley Maidstone sits astride the river, partly in the Weald, partly on the Downs and in the very centre of Kent, and there the Medway changes its course back to north towards Rochester.

All approaches to Maidstone are pleasant. Trees abound. Views continually break upon you. You prepare yourself for a spacious city. You do not find it. Maidstone is congested. It could not be otherwise, for Maidstone is very old, and the buildings of very old towns are almost always clustered close together. That is not a criticism. The compact can hold as much delight as the spacious, but the appeal of the one is absolutely different from the appeal of the other. You cannot compare an expansive city with a town concentrated in half the space.

Maidstone is certainly concentrated. Its streets are full of bustle and business, and that has been its main characteristic for centuries. Daniel Defoe in his *Tour through the Whole Island of Great Britain* wrote that from Maidstone 'and the neighbouring parts London is supplied with more particulars than from any single market town in England'. That was in 1722. Though Maidstone today could not claim a supply business so near monopoly, the picture evoked by Defoe's words is still accurate. Though only thirty-five miles from London, Maidstone is still a commercial centre.

How old is this thriving town? It is referred to in a Saxon document of about AD 975, the *Textus Roffensis*, which called it 'Maegthanstane'. Scholars think that could mean 'maiden's stone' or 'people's stone', more probably the former. *The Oxford Dictionary of English Place Names* also quotes 'maiden's stone' as the most probable derivation, but nobody has so far suggested any reason for the term. One's mind wanders off to Cornwall and the ring of nineteen standing stones near Lamorna, the Merry Maidens. But there is no standing stone at Maidstone.

The *Textus Roffensis* notes that Maidstone belonged to the archbishop of Canterbury. Domesday Book records a manor of fifteen to sixteen hundred acres. In neither the Saxon document nor the Norman register is there any mention of a village, still less a town. But a prosperous town developed during the Middle Ages and steadily grew. The archbishops retained their ownership of it until 1537, when Cranmer did a deal with King Henry VIII, exchanging Maidstone for various other lands, including monastic sites. By that time Maidstone was well established, with a flourishing port, and by 1662 it was considered one of the most prosperous towns in the country.

For the most part, Maidstone's history has been quiet, though there have been rough episodes. Wat Tyler's peasant rebellion swept over the town in 1381 on its way to London, releasing from Maidstone prison *en route* John Ball, author of that shockingly subversive couplet:

When Adam delved and Eve span,
  Who was then the gentleman?

Sixty-nine years later, in 1450, Maidstone backed another rebel, Jack Cade, and in 1554 the town stood four-square behind Sir Thomas Wyatt the Younger in his revolt against Queen Mary's engagement to Philip of Spain. That cost Sir Thomas his head.

The Wyatt family lived at Allington Castle on the western outskirts of Maidstone just south of the river. Wyatt, the rebel against Catholic Mary, was the son of Sir Thomas Wyatt, poet, diplomat and traveller, whose service to his country may have been distinguished but is lightly remembered. His service to English literature, however, is of the greatest significance, for he introduced to England from Italy the sonnet, a poetic form which so exactly suited the English language that it might have been invented particularly for the purpose. Wyatt himself was the first to write an English sonnet, but he expressed his greatest depths of feeling in other forms, holding up a mirror to the intrigue, treachery and power-lust of the age in which he lived, using caustic words just the kinder side of bitterness:

Throughout the world if it were sought,
  Fair words enough a man shall find;
They be good cheap, they cost right nought,
  Their substance is but only wind.
  But well to say, and so to mean,
  That sweet accord is seldom seen.

He called that verse 'Honesty'.

Maidstone is congested but not choked. Streets are not wide, but they are not medieval alleys. In such a town modern multi-storey structures look even more than usually alien. They tower above the close-knit pattern of streets, shops and houses. They are immense yet they look squat and they are devoid of grace. Their impact is greatest at evening, grim silhouettes in the sunset.

Hazlitt, the essayist and critic, was born in one of the little Maidstone ways, Earl Street, in 1778. Andrew Broughton, who also lived in Earl Street, is remembered for something decidedly less pleasant than Hazlitt's writing. He was Roundhead Mayor of

Maidstone during the turbulent years of the middle seventeenth century. He was also clerk of the High Court of Justice, and in that office he read out the death sentence on King Charles I.

Early Maidstone stood on a triangle of rising ground where the River Len joins the Medway. There the archbishops built a group of ragstone buildings, and the town gradually developed a respectful distance away. The group stands there still, dignified and very lovely, at its centre All Saints Church, begun by Archbishop Courtenay in 1395 as a collegiate church. This is one of the finest and largest of English perpendicular churches. Its nave is ninety-three feet wide and it seats fifteen-hundred people. Its eighty-foot tower is massive and has the familiar turret in the corner. The tower once supported a wooden spire a hundred feet high, but lightning destroyed it in 1730.

Archbishop Courtenay also established a College of Priests, a few yards from the church, from an existing building. Down by the river's edge, rising almost directly from it, is the Archbishop's Palace, also begun in the fourteenth century and largely refronted during the reign of Queen Elizabeth I. Then there are the archbishop's stables, which some authorities consider the finest of all the architectural work carried out by the archbishops at Maidstone. This building is now a museum of carriages. Unless you are bored by transport systems of the past, you would be wise to give these carriages a long, unhurried look.

After the hustle and bustle of the main streets of the town, it is pleasant to linger and take your ease in this mellow, ancient quarter where Maidstone originated. Here the clangour of the town is muted and you are aware only of grey walls and red roofs, the soft lap of the river upon its banks and the rustle of leaves in the overhanging trees.

About four miles from the town centre, Leeds Castle, 'the lady's castle', floats romantically on its placid lake in the long valley. Actually, it stands on two islands, and the lake was formed by damming the River Len. The first castle to stand on the site was a Saxon timber structure, which a Norman baron, Robert de Crévecoeur, replaced with a stone castle in 1119. It has changed hands many times during the succeeding centuries, and it has been subjected to many alterations and modifications. It passed to Edward I in 1278 and remained a royal possession for the next three hundred years. Edward gave it to his wife, Eleanor of Castile. Many of his successors to the throne also gave the castle to their wives, and that was how it came to be called 'the lady's castle'. Henry VIII transformed the defensive structure into a palace of considerable beauty. Others carried out further alterations according to their fancies. In 1822 it was modernized but also restored to its medieval appearance. A century later it had fallen into disrepair. In that sad condition it was bought in 1926 by Lady Baillie, who restored it to the state in which you see it now. She established the Leeds Castle Foundation, to whom it passed when she died in 1974. The castle and grounds have been open to the public since 1976.

Now we turn our attention to the raised sandstone ridge which so long barred our view of the North Downs. It runs about eleven miles from Yalding in the west to Boughton Malherbe in the east. Yalding is a large village immediately under the ridge. Three rivers meet here, the Beult and the Teise, which join and flow into the Medway. There are three medieval bridges, one of them a hundred feet long. A spacious, mostly thirteenth-century ragstone church has a square tower with a blue cupola. Edmund Blunden, the poet, lived here as a youth, and his father was master of the local school. His poem 'To Teise, a Stream in Kent' is a sharp corrective to those who know these rivers of the Weald only as placid sheets of water. The Teise may become

Deep-dooming floods and foaming flocks of whirlwaves ...

The orchards go with you as you climb to the ridge from Yalding, but apart from the fruit trees you are in a different countryside, a land of hillsides, sometimes steep, sometimes gradual and rounded. From this high, uneven country came the ragstone which we have noticed so often in the churches and many other buildings in the eastern Weald. The area became known as the ragstone hills. Quarrying ragstone was an industry of the highest importance in the south-east during the later Middle Ages and into the sixteenth century, and Maidstone was its major centre. The stone was transported to Maidstone, then a port, and down the Medway and on to London, where it was used for work at Westminster Abbey and the Palace of Westminster and other important buildings. Some of the most prolific quarries were at Boughton Monchelsea, high on the ridge, where they can still be seen. The view over the lower Weald from this point and nearby is immense. We have just travelled through the countryside spread out below, but you have to remind yourself of it. Looking down upon it, at the orchards and the carefully tilled land, you feel curiously apart, and yet, in a contradictory sort of way, also akin.

The village, more of a hamlet really, consists of a church built in the sixteenth century but damaged by fire in 1832, Boughton Monchelsea Place, a sixteenth-century manor house largely reconstructed in the nineteenth, and some cottages.

The other villages on the ridge are also small, with one outstanding exception, Sutton Valence, which is both large and compact. I have even heard it described as a small town. It is not typical of any kind of Wealden village. For that matter, it is not typically English. It is a great surprise. It is built on terraces on the hillside. You might almost be in a mountain village of the southern Mediterranean, overlooking olive groves and vineyards instead of apples, pears and cherries. The terrace roads are necessarily narrow, and traffic must go slowly, so you can stroll about in comfort, ignoring the main road to Tenterden, A274, which slithers down the hillside at the western end of the village. Houses and cottages seem to have been sited individually beside the roads all at the same time. In fact, their diversity in age is great. So are the architecture, style and size. Yet there is no discord in these variations. On the contrary, they add interest to a cohesive whole. There is no single attraction in particular in this unusual place. Simply to be there is enough, particularly when blossom covers the plain below and the fragrant south wind touches your face.

At Ulcombe and Boughton Malherbe you are firmly in England. At Boughton Malherbe a very English farm crowns the top of the ridge, next to a ragstone church whose partly thirteenth-century tower looks like a castle from the level land below. Here this eastern end of the ridge declines in long slopes of grass down to the plain.

The highly uncomplimentary-sounding name means exactly what it says: evil herb. But anything evil seems very unlikely in this quiet, secluded village. Cattle and sheep feed safely on the pastures and are not poisoned by toxic plants invading the meadows. Nor are gardens infiltrated by any such hostile vegetation. The name, however, does not refer to the village but to the name of a family, Malherbe, which is no less puzzling and sounds even more sinister.

The countryside at this end of the ridge is subtly different from the countryside at the western end. Although the orchards are not far off, there are none on the high land round the village. Instead, you find mixed farming of livestock and corn, less intensive than fruit growing, less colourful, but more open. It is a green land, dotted about with hawthorn bushes and spreading, free-standing trees. In summer at harvest time the green is contrasted with the stiff, flaxen heads of wheat and the bowed heads of barley.

Below, the green continues as a flat plain towards Ashford, which is about nine miles off to the south-east. From the lip of a steep descent near the church you can clearly follow the line of the North Downs as they make their final sweeping curve south-east to the cliffs of Folkestone and Dover.

Ulcombe manages to be partly ragstone village and partly Low Weald, but the view from it is almost as memorable as the prospect from Boughton Malherbe. In the church, ragstone of course, there are some impressive wall paintings. The building is of the thirteenth and fourteenth centuries and there are traces of a Norman predecessor. The name of the village, like Boughton Malherbe, is something of a puzzle but the solution is much more pleasant. You won't find it unless you have some knowledge of Anglo-Saxon. It means the valley of the owl – Old english, *ule*.

Now we will leave the ragstone countryside and turn west to that most English of towns, Tunbridge Wells. We shall pass near territory we have already visited but we do not retrace our steps. The little lanes offer plenty of variety, and in our leisurely way we shall in due course arrive at Pembury, a village with a big green and, a mile and a half from the village, a small sandstone church originally Norman but with fourteenth century additions, including a short tower. A new church, also of sandstone, was built in 1846. The village is now almost part of Tunbridge Wells, but stubbornly maintains its independence.

Though we are on the doorstep of Tunbridge Wells, we are still not quite ready to go into the town. First, we will go west a little and spend some time in Southborough, once a village but now virtually part of the famous spa. It is busy but pleasant, and its seventy-five acre common and nearby woods are restful places. Iron was once mined in the area, and a forge was working until 1772.

Now we will pass on to Royal Tunbridge Wells.

4

Tunbridge Wells

A young English nobleman, Dudley, 3rd Baron North, was riding back to London from Eridge Park, where he had been a guest of Lord Bergavenny. He disliked Eridge. He disliked its loneliness and its quietude and he disliked its lack of any amusement. In fact, he disliked the countryside and was in it only because his doctor had advised him to shake off the effects of dissipated, fashionable London by breathing country air. But Lord North found breathing country air unpleasant, country views an affront to his vision and the whole thing unutterably boring. He yearned for the busy streets of London, the familiar cries, the drinking and gambling, the swift give and take of city discourse. He wanted to go back, and why shouldn't he and be damned to the physicians? It was his life and not theirs and if he stayed out here he would die of boredom anyway. So they saddled up his horse and back he started, careless of the danger to his health, which was probably not all that serious, for there was a certain rivalry in ailments at the time, which was 1609, and a great vogue in cures and waters.

About three miles from Eridge Lord North noticed a wayside spring with a brownish-yellow deposit round it. Such ocherous deposits are sediments from iron enriched water, produced by rainfall seeping through the iron-laced soil, so plentiful in the Weald. Lord North reined in his horse. He remembered that kind of deposit. He had seen it at the famous chalybeate spa in Germany. He dismounted and, borrowing a cup from a cottager called Mrs Humphreys, he took a drink of the water from the spring. He was instantly convinced that it contained healing properties. His opinion was endorsed by medical experts to whom he took samples for analysis, and that was the beginning of Royal Tunbridge Wells.

North was not one to keep things to himself, and in a very short while visitors began to cluster round the spring. Lord Bergavenny cleared trees away from it, for it was on his estate, sank a well over it and built a pavement round it. It became the object of pilgrimage for health-seekers. Presently so many fashionable invalids, real and imaginary, flocked to the spot that accommodation in the neighbourhood could not cope.

Its social significance rose rapidly. The year 1630 brought the first royal visit. Henrietta Maria, Queen of Charles I, went to the 'wells' after the birth of her son, the future Charles II. The Queen and her entourage camped in tents on a nearby common for six weeks and then returned to London 'much improved'.

But the idea of the Queen in a tent shocked the residents of the neighbourhood into doing something for the comfort of the aristocratic ladies and gentleman who were arriving in such numbers to 'take the waters'. Hotels and lodging-houses began to appear. There was a great surge of planned development after the Civil War which ravaged England from 1642 to 1649. The restoration of Charles II in 1660 provided an even greater impetus. When, in the mid-1660s, the King himself arrived with his Queen Catherine, he found a very different place from the 'wells' his mother had visited just over thirty years before. Tunbridge Wells had become a fashionable resort with a 'season' lasting from May to October. Beautiful buildings had appeared and pleasant walks had been laid out, the precursors of the famous Pantiles. There were two walks in particular, the upper and the lower. The upper was the fashionable promenade, covered and colonnaded in 1638. The lower was the place to which country people brought their produce for sale. Few of the people who went there needed any health-restoring waters. They were vigorous, vivacious, loving life, eager to take advantage of the many entertainments now liberally provided. Of course, they could still take the waters if they wished, and most did. You can yourself.

Princess Anne, later Queen Anne, became a regular visitor. So did Princess Victoria, and when she became Queen she took her consort, Prince Albert, with her. Visiting royal dukes and duchesses were almost too numerous to count, and the church of King Charles the Martyr, built in the 1670s and 1680s, commemorated this famous and tragic monarch. The church is renowned for the beauty of its plaster ceilings.

In a roundabout way it was due to Princess Anne that the

Pantiles came by their name. In 1698 her son, the Duke of Gloucester, slipped on the unpaved upper walk, so she provided £100 to have the surface properly paved. But nothing had been done when she returned the following year. She was deeply offended and went away and never came back. Two years later the inhabitants paved the walks at their own expense with square tiles called pantiles. Today you walk on Purbeck flagstones which replaced the pantiles towards the end of the eighteenth century, but a few of the original tiles remain by the spring, long since decorously housed.

By the end of the seventeenth century Tunbridge Wells had become one of the most fashionable places in the country, probably *the* most fashionable outside London, certainly so in the summer 'season', when it became the rival of Bath, which it eventually superseded. But it would be entirely wrong to suppose that Tunbridge Wells or Bath either, for that matter, existed solely to provide amusement for the idle and the bored rich, searching for something to fill empty and not very intelligent minds. Large numbers of the visitors to Tunbridge Wells were anything but idle, and they included some of the highest intelligences in the kingdom. If not all things to all men, it was very many things to many different kinds of people. John Evelyn, the diarist, saw it as 'a very sweet place, private and refreshing'. Politicians and diplomats saw it as a kind of London transported to the country. The dissipated saw it as a place where they could indulge themselves without restraint. The ailing and the invalids saw it as a place where they could get better.

Into this glittering assembly of influence, talent and whim drove Beau Nash in 1735. He came as the town's first Master of Ceremonies, and he deserted Bath to do so. Nash, the 'king of fashion' in his day, had a deep and lasting effect on Tunbridge Wells, but he did not create the town as a centre of fashion or political thought, or as a watering place. It was already all of these things. What Nash did was to develop them, and he did this with outstanding success. During his reign there were few famous people who did not visit the town. They included Garrick, the actor, William Pitt the Elder and Samuel Richardson, the novelist. There was never a dull moment in a day which began early and ended late. Nash insisted on strict rules which sometimes seemed almost a time-table. If visitors wanted to drink the waters, they had to do it between 7 a.m. and 9 a.m. After that they haunted the coffee-houses and the gaming-rooms, they drank tea and drank wine. They gossiped, they scandalized and they gambled. But they also spent a lot of time in the bookshops, and they went riding and walking in a countryside which is still as beautiful as it was in their day. Music and balls followed in the evening, and then for many the night was given to love. Yet, so far as I can see, nobody ever admitted to the slightest weariness.

Nash died in 1761 but the brilliance of the town continued undiminished. Edmund Kean, Charles Kemble and William Dowton appeared in a newly built theatre. Thackeray stayed for several months at a house on the London road, where he wrote 'Tunbridge Toys', one of a series of essays called collectively 'Roundabout Papers' and published in the *Cornhill Magazine* which he edited. But that was not until 1860, when Tunbridge Wells had passed its zenith and was sinking in a kind of evening afterglow.

The first faint signs of decline began to appear before the eighteenth century was out. The main reason was a new rival, a place called Brighthelmstone on the Sussex coast, soon to be abbreviated to Brighton. Just as Tunbridge Wells superseded Bath, so now Brighton threatened to supersede Tunbridge Wells and eventually did so. It had been discovered that bathing in the sea and breathing in sea air did you good. The distance from London, fifty-two miles, was of little concern because the new fast stage-coaches got you down to the coast in about ten hours. Brighton rose to unchallenged supremacy when the Prince Regent, later King George IV, made the little seaside town his favourite retreat.

Tunbridge Wells faded as a resort, but with the coming of the railway it grew rapidly as a residential and business centre. Ironically, it also recovered a great deal of its old health-spa status, which invested it with a reputation for stuffiness in the nineteenth century. The flamboyance never returned. The Pantiles grew decrepit and deserted. The shops and the cafés moved to the developing and bustling business area. But the grace of the original Tunbridge Wells never completely vanished, and today its popularity has returned, particularly among visitors, both British and overseas, who throng the cleaned-up Pantiles. You hear tongues of many nations as you stroll beside the colonnade, or enjoy your aperitif or tea or coffee in the bars of cafés or, on a nice day, in the open air in the sunshine. There is no traffic to trouble you. If you fancy a sip from the spring you will certainly taste the iron.

The common where Queen Henrietta Maria had to camp reaches down to the town and almost touches the Pantiles. There are over 250 acres of mingled grass and woodland, not thrust into an urban straitjacket, trimmed, mown, pruned and lopped, but more or less left to grow as it likes, within reason.

The whole town is stamped with a certain elegance, and it still wears an air of dignified unhaste. It has been affectionately described as the international tourists' haven. I have always found friendliness there.

The prefix 'Royal' did not come into use until far on in the town's history and a very long time after the necessary qualifications, you might suppose, had been achieved. In 1909 the mayor and burgesses of Tunbridge Wells petitioned King Edward VII to add 'Royal' to the name of the town. The King had visited the town in 1881 as Prince of Wales, but the petition was made not because of any particular royal association or occasion but because of so many. They were all matters of history, and the King had no need to give the request any great amount of consideration; he just granted it. I like to think he murmured to himself, 'And about time, too; I must go back.' But he never did.

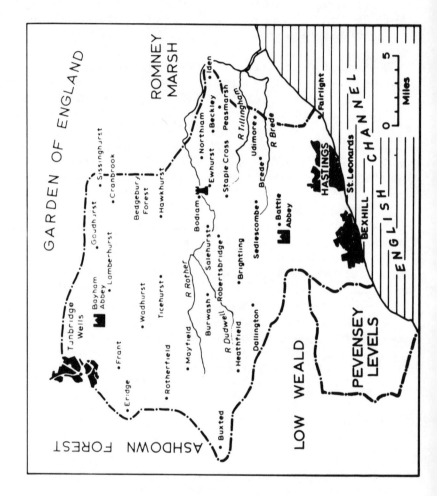

The High Weald

5

The High Weald

Tunbridge Wells marks the junction of three distinct areas, the highly cultivated region we have just explored, the North Weald and the High Weald, which is a tumbled land of green hills, green valleys, forest and pasture. It is a land unto itself, and we shall now set out to explore it. You meet some oasthouses, hop gardens and orchards, but they do not look at home. They seem to have strayed from the industrious region to the east which is given over altogether to food production, as we have seen. The countryside we are just entering is not unproductive, but it is less intensive. Man goes hand in hand with nature here. There is more wildlife: more birds, more animals, more wild plant life. In the evening or early morning you may well see a fallow or roe deer. Yet nowhere is the landscape really wild. The nearest you get to wilderness is in Forestry Commission woodlands, where wildlife is encouraged and timber is cultivated. This aspect of the Commissions' work is too often overlooked. It is vital. Wild creatures, banished by housing, industrial development and intensive agriculture, find new habitats in the forests and open spaces held by the Commission, for by no means all its land is covered by trees.

It is a cared-for countryside, dependent entirely on man for its appearance. It is largely livestock country, comprising many small to medium-sized farms with grass very evident, interspersed among the woodlands and grown as leys in a rotation, as on Romney Marsh. The hilly land holds the moisture, and the grass is a deep, verdant green. It is one of my pleasures to find a high place in this tumbled landscape and look down the long valleys where white sheep and red, amber or black-and-white cattle graze the grass, and sunlight and cloud shadows pass slowly from valley to hill.

It is a country of outstanding beauty, singularly quiet and little visited except in one or two places celebrated for their historic or literary associations. Its structure is sandstone liberally bespattered with pockets of clay, and it stretches about thirty-five miles south-east to end abruptly in the tawny cliffs of Hastings and Fairlight. Narrow and winding lanes thread their way through the valleys and over the hills, connecting villages which for the most part lie almost unseen in valleys but occasionally stand prominently on hilltops. From time to time the lanes emerge from the meadowland and woods to cross a main road, which, however, is soon forgotten as once more woods and grassy banks close upon you, shutting off the stream of traffic from your vision, softening its noise upon your ears. Sweet chestnut mingles with hazel, beech with oak and ash, alders overhang little streams, and there must be more windmills per square mile in this region than anywhere else in the country. Many have been rescued from decay and even near ruin, and today stand as proudly on their hilltops as ever they did. Their white paint catches the light, so that they are easily recognizable landmarks from far distances.

But it is a vulnerable landscape. Intelligent conservation has maintained and even enhanced its delicately balanced beauty, but the constitution of local authorities changes frequently. A brash attitude of mind, bent on 'opening up' the area, could very quickly entirely destroy its particular appeal. From time to time there are murmurs about its potential attraction as a tourist area, and indeed it could easily become a visitors' playground, with hotels, 'discreetly sited' of course, equally 'discreet' parking places for cars and coaches, 'discreetly' widened roads and 'discreet' advertising, leading to the 'discreet' and complete annihilation of the special character of the region. Tourism need not clash with agriculture and forestry, but it often does and it would certainly do so here if practised on a wide commercial scale. Many visitors, both British and overseas, already enjoy happy holidays in this secluded stretch of the Weald, but they come as individuals and not as packaged parties, and part of their pleasure is to savour the everyday work which maintains the countryside as they know it and as they would wish it to remain.

Though there is not much open country, there are many footpaths, and it is also pleasant to walk the lanes, for they are comparatively free of traffic. You can, of course, drive along them, but a lot of concentration is necessary on these narrow, twisting

River Medway at Maidstone

Prospect from Boughton Malherbe, where the sandstone ridge under the North Downs declines in long slopes of grass

Old Palace, Brenchley. The front is not old but a skilled restoration

Apple-blossom time at Brenchley

ways. Often two cars can pass only with difficulty and sometimes not at all, so that one driver must reverse to a passing place. I find this no hardship, but you do miss a lot, the flowers on the banks, for instance, because you must so carefully watch where you are going. There is much to be said for travelling on a bicycle, but you should be prepared to push a lot, for hills are steep, long and numerous, a circumstance which put ire into the sold of E.V. Lucas, author of *Highways and Byways of Sussex*, and prompted him to complain about this 'switchback district' and 'fatiguing country', where no sooner had you reached one hilltop than you were faced with another.

This up-and-down country is the land of the 'hursts', derived from '*hyrst*', Old English for hillock or knoll, especially of a sandy nature, or copse, wood or wooded hill. These are familiar features through the length of the region. You find the term all over the Weald, as either a prefix or a suffix, but you meet it most often in the villages of this area of highland and lowland, and most frequently at its northern end, where there is a positive constellation of hursts within a small circumference.

Two towns dominate the region, Cranbrook in the north and Battle in the south. They are about twenty-two miles apart and utterly dissimilar.

The white weatherboards of Cranbrook gleam brightly in the sun and only slightly less brightly in the rain. They are the main characteristic of the town. There are both new and old weatherboarded buildings, and all are maintained with meticulous care. They stand close together, so that they make an immediate and deep impression on the mind. When you reach the town's outskirts, you feel you are about to drive into a white city, and this feeling remains with you when you are actually in the place, although stone buildings mingle with the weatherboarded structures.

The most prominent of these weatherboarded buildings is also the most prominent building in the town, which it entirely dominates. It is a white smock windmill, Union Mill, and it seems to float above the streets, houses and business premises, seventy-two feet high, including a brick base. It is in perfect condition, complete with sweeps, bonnet-like cap and fantail, and it cost £3,500 when it was built in 1814. You continually catch glimpses of it as you walk about the town, and when you turn into Stone Street it completes a sudden vista, for the long street seems to lead straight up to the mill. A windmill in the middle of a town is unexpected to say the least, but not here. It looks perfectly at home.

Visitors always want to know how it came by its unusual name. Its first miller was Henry Dobell, for whom it was built, but after five years, in 1819, Dobell went bankrupt. His creditors got together, formed a 'union' and ran the mill until 1832. Then George and John Russell bought it, and the family Russell ran it until 1958, when Kent County Council became its trustees.

Were it not for the mill, the church would be Cranbrook's most conspicuous building. It is a noble piece of architecture, and it is often called 'the Cathedral of the Weald'. It is also a church of great beauty, both inside and out. The builders started about the middle of the fourteenth century, using the local sandstone and not the ragstone of which so many of the churches in this part of the Weald were built. Work continued for the next two hundred years, and scarcely anything has been changed, modified, 'improved' or, worse still, restored, since the last stone was laid in the middle of the sixteenth century. The roof is an exception, and that was unlucky. In 1866 the existing roof was found to be so badly decayed that a wholesale renewal was essential. The replacement is claimed to be an exact replica of the sixteenth-century original.

You are struck by two things when you look at the church from the churchyard. One is the powerful tower, seventy-four feet high, completed by 1425, with a stone figure of Father Time and his scythe on the south face. The other is the abundance of windows. They are lovely to look at, but that is not their prime function. When you go into the church you are immediately aware of an all-pervading soft but clear light which emphasizes the spaciousness of the building. The high clerestory windows are a potent influence and, in the even spread of the light, arches and fluted pillars take your eye up to the timbered roof. You are not dwarfed by the expanse of this beautiful interior. The dignity of the architecture, the cool, uncluttered stone and freedom from impediment to movement, impart a sense of belonging.

Cranbrook church has a dipping font, or pool, for baptism by total immersion. It was built by the Reverend John Johnson in 1710 to placate the large number of Baptists in the parish. But only one such baptism is recorded.

The church must have cost a lot of money, first to build and then to maintain; but Cranbrook was a wealthy town, thanks to the cloth-manufacturers, who made it one of their most important centres. Queen Elizabeth I visited the town in 1573 and watched cloth-making in progress, and there is a story that she walked the mile from the fifteenth-century George Hotel to the manor house at Coursehorne on Cranbrook broadcloth specially woven for the purpose.

During this visit Elizabeth granted a charter to Cranbrook school, setting out that, 'Within the Parish of Cranbrook there shall hereafter be for ever a certain free and perpetual Grammar School and that the same school shall hereafter for ever be called the free and perpetual Grammar School of Queen Elizabeth in Cranbrook.' The present buildings are of the eighteenth, nineteenth and twentieth centuries.

Woodland and pasture press close to the walls of Cranbrook's houses, and you are aware of this even in the busy town centre. Yet, ironically, it was industrial pollution which brought within a few miles of Cranbrook a forestry project which developed into both national and international importance.

Early in the 1920s the authorities at the Royal Botanic Gardens, Kew, realized with alarm that the conifers in the Gardens faced disaster through poison in the air. They called a conference with the Forestry Commission to see what could be done, if anything, to combat the impurities in the London atmosphere. The result was depressing. The conference decided that nothing could be done for Kew's standing trees, and any thoughts of a rescue operation were abandoned. But the upshot was not surrender but a fresh approach. Since Kew's mature conifers seemed doomed, would it be possible to ensure healthy growth for conifers of the future by establishing a pinetum on Commission land where the air was cleaner? A search (how delightful that must have been) resulted in the selection of a site on the western edge of Bedgebury Forest about four miles from Cranbrook.

Planting began in 1925 under the joint administration of the Botanic Gardens and the Commission, and as work progressed it became clear that this was going to be something far more ambitious than an alternative to a polluted part of Kew. The foresters were establishing a living collection of fir trees more comprehensive than anything else of its kind in the country. Today these trees, grown up, constitute the National Pinetum of Great Britain, now entirely the responsibility of the Commission. It covers eighty acres. It is first and foremost a place for scientific study, and scientists and students from all over the world visit it. But it is also a place for enjoyment and it is open to the public all the year round free of charge. Much of its charm lies in its informality. The natural undulations of the land have been made the most of. So has a big lake which lies at the northern tip of the reserve. This is a tranquil spot, surrounded not only by firs but also by the trees which are natives of the Weald. Oaks spread their rugged boughs above the banks. Willows and birches lean over and sweep the water with lace-like branches. Swallows skim the lake just above water-lilies.

Every type of conifer that grows in Britain is to be found in the pinetum, and there are also specimens of cone-bearing trees from pretty well all the temperate regions of the world. Where they stand depends upon their shape and size. Column-shaped trees, for instance, look well upon a hilltop. Dwarf or small spreading trees are exactly right for banks overlooking valleys. Areas are named according to the trees they support. You might find yourself in Cypress Valley or on top of Pine Hill or walking beside Yew Bank – and what variety of colour and size there is among the yews. Luxuriant ferns and other moisture-loving plants grow on the banks of two streams which feed the lake.

I think the impression that lasts longest after a visit to this magnificent collection is the range of colour. Apart from the multi-coloured yews, there are silver greens and blue greens, emeralds and golds, mingling with ordinary, everyday greens, also in notable variety. In spring they are all set off by a blaze of rhododendrons and azaleas; and in the autumn by reds, russets, golds and yellows of the native deciduous trees.

Bedgebury Forest covers about 2,470 acres and is historically an ancient place. It was part of the manor of Bedgebury, mentioned in a deed of Kenwulf, King of Mercia, in AD 815. The forest you see today, however, owes little to natural regeneration and practically everything to replanting. The two world wars took an enormous toll, and a disastrous fire in 1942 devastated over 360 acres. In its reclamation programme the Commission planted both broadleaved trees and conifers, and you can wander where you like, but the Commission makes an urgent appeal to visitors not to do anything that could start a fire. An eighty-foot steel look-out tower has eased the foresters' apprehensions a little; nevertheless, fires cannot always be detected soon enough to smother them before they take a firm hold.

There is another Commission forest two miles east of Cranbrook called Hempstead Forest. It covers about a thousand acres and is also open to the public. Here, too, the fear of fire is always present, despite another helpful tower.

Both forests are interspersed with meadowland where you can stand back, detached, and look at the trees, quite a different thing from being among them. From such standpoints in the evening you watch the level rays of the sinking sun pick out individual trees from the mass. Beeches, oaks, pines and birch are suddenly, for a few moments, brilliantly illuminated. Then shadows spread upwards, the brilliance fades, and soon only the leaves of the topmost branches catch the light.

The region of the High Weald held the biggest concentrations of the iron-smelting centres in the Weald. Here was the very heart of the Wealden iron industry, and you are reminded of it not by the names of the villages, which are much older than the furnaces, but by place-names of a more local and intimate nature such as Furnace Farm, Furnace Wood, Forge Farm and Cinder Hill.

For generations, many of the villages led a dual life, cloth-making and iron-casting overlapping, but eventually iron became paramount. Both sight and sound of the industry were ever present among the hills and valleys. The furnaces glowed both night and day, the gigantic hammers thumped, the trees fell. The thickly wooded countryside changed out of recognition as the trees crashed in increasing numbers to provide charcoal fuel to feed the insatiable furnaces. The ironmasters found a highly profitable market in the manufacture of cannon both for England's armed forces and for those of other countries.

But eventually the destruction of the forest created alarm among the nation's leaders. A statute was passed in the reign of Henry VIII ordering that there should be left in every acre 'twelve standels or stores or oak'. An Act in the reign of his daughter Queen Elizabeth I forbade timber-felling to produce iron. The Admiralty acidly pointed out that felling on this scale to make cannon would soon result in insufficient timber to build ships. But the felling went on.

Yet the Wealden iron industry, even at its most concentrated, did not produce anything like the filth, ugliness and human degradation of the nineteenth-century Black Country in the Midlands and the North. There is a world of difference between the belching chimneys fed by coal and the spirals of charcoal smoke which signalled the cremation of the Weald. There are no unsightly relics of bygone heavy industry in the villages and the landscape of the High Weald, or, for that matter, anywhere else in the Weald; just an elusive feeling of something significant long since departed. In fact, the Wealden iron industry has actually enriched the countryside through the bequest of large numbers of hammer ponds. These ponds were often sizeable and even large lakes. They were created to provide water power to operate large bellows for the furnaces and massive hammers to beat the iron ore. They are with us still, but now they are tranquil stretches of water, usually surrounded by trees, beloved of anglers, waterfowl and those who just want a little peace and quiet.

Goudhurst, pronounced 'Gowdhurst' with the '-ow' as in 'how', is often called the capital of the hurst villages. It has the air of a small town, a broad main street stretching up a steep hill from a decorative pond at the bottom to a sandstone church on top with a short but sturdy tower, built about the middle of the seventeenth century. It replaced an earlier tower destroyed by fire a century earlier. Much of the church is thirteenth and fourteenth century, and the minute you set foot inside you are aware simultaneously of airiness and light, monuments and brasses. Most are to the Culpepers, the most powerful family in this part of the Weald until the late seventeenth century.

Houses between church and pond are a fascinating mixture, a planner's nightmare but loved by artists. The town ran prosperous enterprises in both cloth and iron.

If Goudhurst is the capital of the hursts, Sissinghurst is by far the best known owing to its 'castle'. It was taken over in 1930 by

Victoria Sackville-West and Sir Harold Nicolson, who found not a castle but a derelict Elizabethan mansion. Most people would have blanched at the very idea of doing anything with it, but not this pair. Out of the incompatible mass of masonry, together, man and wife, they created a home; around their home they created a garden, and this is what people go to see. It is an outstanding garden, in which formality and informality merge happily together.

Sissinghurst Castle, now owned by the National Trust, is not quite on the high land, not quite on the low plain to the east, but somewhere between the two. From her home Miss Sackville-West could contemplate the low land, its cantakerous clay, its orchards and its little meadows, and every Wealden farmer will appreciate deep in his heart her words from her long poem *The Land*:

But only a bold man ploughs the Weald for corn,
Most are content with fruit or pasture, knowing
Too well both drought and winter's heavy going.

Ironworks at Lamberhurst, four miles west of Goudhurst, had the distinction of casting railings for St Paul's Cathedral, perhaps with the co-operation of other furnaces. They weighed two hundred tons. The village, a compact place of varied architecture and age, climbs a hill from a bridge over the River Teise. It was once quiet and secluded but the build-up of traffic in recent years has brought much noise. Despite that, Lamberhurst retains an air of dignified withdrawal, and you have the impression that the rushing metal is merely a temporary nuisance.

Two ancient buildings, Scotney Castle and Bayham Abbey, are near the village. Scotney, like Sissinghurst, is graced by beautiful gardens. The Hussey family landscaped them in the 1840s with the remains of the moated fourteenth-century castle as the focal point. The ruins, flowers, shrubs and grass strongly appealed to Rose Macaulay, who wrote in *Pleasure of Ruins* that, 'Sky and trees, against a steep wilderness of quarry and towers today make an exquisite picture.'

The ruins of Bayham Abbey stand in perfect peace beside the waters of the Teise. It so deeply impressed Richard Church that he says in his book *Kent* that he found difficulty in writing about it, adding, simply, 'Its beauty is absolute.' It was founded early in the thirteenth century by Robert de Turneham and Ela de Sackville, and it was occupied by the strict Premonstratension Order, whose mother abbey was at Prémonstré, in Aisne.

A six-mile journey through thick plantations brings you to Frant, partly grouped about a green far more extensive than at first appears, and partly flanking the busy A267 road to Eastbourne. It is a kind of plateau, five hundred feet above sea-level westward, it overlooks Eridge Park, and north, a wide valley to the rooftops of Tunbridge Wells. A large and imposing church, rebuilt in 1821, reminds you that you are in the Wealden iron country, for the piers of the nave are not stone but iron. A tablet commemorates Colonel John By, who founded Ottawa, first called Bytown. He died at Shernfield Park, near the village, in 1836, and is buried in the churchyard.

Southward, Rotherfield crowns another five-hundred-foot hill, overlooking the valley of the River Rother, which rises nearby and gives the village its name. Where the hill curves highest stands the church, in the centre of the village. Its tall, shingled spire is a landmark over great tracts of the Weald. It is a handsome building mostly of the thirteenth century, mostly stone. The tower, later, fifteenth century, is a stout piece of work and needs to be to support that spire. Murals on the interior walls are rather faint but clear enough for their quality to be appreciated. They were probably painted when the church was built, and almost certainly covered the entire walls, telling the Biblical stories in the only possible way at that time, for the people could not read.

This church succeeded several wooden structures, probably three. The original was built by a Saxon chief, Duke Berhtwald, about AD 780, in thanksgiving for recovery from illness. He dedicated it to St Dionysios, and this dedication has remained with a slight modification, St Denys.

Rotherfield has almost as much the air of a town as a village, and you have to be careful crossing the road. All the same, it is a place for strolling, and frequently through gaps between the houses, or through an archway, you catch tantalizing glimpses of far vistas in this land of hills and valleys. A post-mill stands on the six-hundred-foot crest of one of these green heights, Argos Hill, about a mile from the village. The date of its building is uncertain, but it worked until 1927 and then gradually fell into decay. It has been carefully restored and is now as dramatic a landmark as its companion at Cranbrook.

Rotherfield stands on a loop of the B2101, off the A267, and this saves it from the worst of the London-Eastbourne traffic. Mayfield, however, sits astride the main road about three miles south-east, and the volume of traffic can reduce you to deafened weariness. The revving-up of the cars and the clatter of trucks seems sometimes incessant, and you cover your nostrils to escape the smells of exhaust. Yet if the nineteenth-century poet Coventry Patmore could come back, he would probably not change his mind that Mayfield is 'the sweetest village in England'. The best way to approach it is not from the Rotherfield end but from the south. Then you see it almost as a southern European hill village, flowing down from the church on the topmost point. It is a splendid picture when the morning sun plays upon the flank of the hill.

It is a big and ancient village, and its long high street is rich in oak timber work. Your attention is riveted by the timber-framed sixteenth-century Middle House, now a hotel; nor could you miss the beautiful house next door, more than a hundred years older.

Mayfield is deeply imbued with legends of St Dunstan, Archbishop of Canterbury from 960 to 988. He was born at Mayfield but brought up at Glastonbury. He is said to have built a wooden church at Mayfield, where, says a legend, he also pinched the devil's nose with red-hot tongs, a feat, however, which is also claimed to have been performed at Glastonbury.

St Dunstan also founded a palace for the archbishops of Canterbury at Mayfield. Archbishop Simon Islip completely rebuilt it in the fourteenth century and included a banqueting hall of great splendour and architectural merit. Thomas Cranmer was the last archbishop to own the palace. He made it over to King Henry VIII in 1545. Then it passed from hand to hand and eventually fell into ruin and became a quarry for local builders. Stones from it can be recognized in buildings in the village and neighbourhood. It might well have disintegrated altogether had it not been for the Duchess of Leeds and Mother Cornelia Connelly, founder of the Society of the Holy Child. The Duchess, an American lady, bought the palace remains in 1863 and gave them to the Society on condition that they were properly restored. That would have been enough to daunt most people, but not the redoubtable Mother Cornelia, also American. She instigated a determined European whip-round and raised enough money to carry out a thorough and tasteful restoration. Where the archbishops had stayed she established a convent, and the great hall became the convent chapel. In *Sussex (Buildings of England* series) Nikolaus Pevsner considers this half to be 'one of the most spectacular medieval halls of England'. The well-known Mayfield convent school, opened in 1872, is next door to the convent itself.

The church, within yards of the palace, is as imposing at close quarters as from the distance and is naturally dedicated to St Dunstan. Most of it dates from the early fifteenth century, a rebuilding of an older church which was badly damaged in a fire which swept through the village in 1389. The palace and the thirteenth-century church tower escaped. Iron grave slabs let into the pavement of the nave and the chancel commemorate the families of local ironmasters and are the work of local furnaces.

The origin of the village's pretty name is in doubt. There are several possibilities to choose from. The most likely seems to be a field where mayweed grew (Saxon Maghefeld). But the village signs prefers the more romantic 'maid's field' and shows the maid with two attendants. It also shows St Dunstan with tongs giving the devil his due.

The village stands on the lip of the Rother Valley, and from some of the gardens you seem to be looking down a steep gorge.

The best known of all the iron-smelting centres was Buxted, not because it turned out more products but because ironmaster Ralph Hogge, at his Buxted furnace in 1543, cast the first English cannon in one piece. To celebrate the event somebody wrote this awful couplet:

Master Huggett and his man John
They did make the first cannon.

There is no record that Master Huggett had a man John, but the writer had to make his lines rhyme somehow.

Buxted is about six miles west of Mayfield; slightly north-east, three hursts are strung in line on a high ridge, west to east, Wadhurst, Ticehurst and Hawkhurst. Wadhurst and Ticehurst were very deeply involved in the iron industry, Hawkhurst in a much more hazardous occupation, smuggling.

Wadhurst is distinctly more town than village and was, in fact, granted a charter in 1253 by King Henry III, who conferred the right to hold a weekly market and an annual fair. A weekly livestock market is still held on Monday. The name is pure Saxon, Wada's hyrst (wood).

Wadhurst is probably the oldest of all the Wealden iron-smelting centres and one of the most important. The Celts mined iron ore at several centres here, and there is little doubt that the Romans encouraged them to carry on. There was certainly a Roman ironworks between Wadhurst and Ticehurst, and a Roman trackway led east along the ridge down to Newenden, where iron could have been shipped. Westward the track led to Frant and then north to London.

Exactly how important Wadhurst was as an iron centre can be assessed by a visit to the church, where you will find thirty-one fine cast-iron memorial floor slabs and one more in the churchyard. They span a period of over 180 years, from 1617 to 1799.

Wadhurst gave up its iron industry with great reluctance and not without a struggle. Long after all the Wealden furnaces had closed, including its own, Wadhurst opened new mines in Snapes wood, about a mile from the little town. It was in August 1857. As all the furnaces in the neighbourhood had gone out, the ore was sent to Staffordshire for smelting. It was a gallant attempt but it stood little chance of success. The mines were closed almost exactly a year later, in September 1858, but they are still to be seen, in the wood.

Wadhurst is a place of character, a bright and sparkling place. Shops in pleasant variety line the long high street, and all sorts of architectural styles greet you, red tile, white weatherboards, grey stone and mellow sandstone, wavy roofs and straight roofs. Though it stands in a green and quiet recess, the church is nevertheless the most prominent building. A slender shingled spire rests on a Norman tower and rises 128 feet from the ground. The rest of the building grew from the thirteenth century to the sixteenth, replacing original twelfth-century work. The evening sun plays upons the spire when twilight has claimed the rest of the church and most of the town, and it gleams like illuminated silver.

Ticehurst has a strong focus, the square, pleasantly shaded by chestnut trees. A fifteenth-century coaching inn, the Bell, instantly catches the eye at one side of the square. The prettiest corners of the small town are round the sandstone and fourteenth-century church. There are attractive lines of gables and intriguing little ways, half concealed, among white weatherboarded houses. Traffic cannot pass along these lanes and you often feel you are walking down a private drive. The remains of a Roman bloomery at Holbeamwood, two miles off, were excavated in 1968.

Man made a dramatic impact on the landscape between the two towns with the construction of a huge reservoir, the largest single sheet of inland water between London and the coast. It was built by the Southern Water Authority and the Mid Kent Water Company, and it supplies water to the North Kent and Maidstone areas. It is called the Bewl Bridge Reservoir. It took three years to complete, from 1973 to 1976, it holds 6,900 million gallons, the area of water is 770 acres and the distance round the perimeter is 15 miles. But the big lake is not a boring rectangle or oval. Its outline is pleasingly irregular, and long arms reach into the surrounding pastures. On the map it looks rather like Poseidon's trident. The reservoir is supplied by the River Bewl, by a number of streams and by water pumped into it along a three-mile pipeline from the Teise at Smallbridge. The water is confined by a dam across the Bewl a thousand yards long and over a hundred feet high in the centre.

The whole project is an impressive piece of engineering skill, and the two authorities also realized that such a large stretch of water and the surrounding countryside offered opportunities for recreation on an extensive scale. They took full advantage of these potentials. At Bewl Bridge you can sail, dive, row, canoe, fish, walk and ride. You can also sit quietly and watch waterbirds, for the central prong of the reservoir is set aside as a nature reserve and is managed by the Sussex Trust for Nature Conservation. You must, however, have a permit before you can visit this area, where wildlife takes precedence.

There are extensive car-parks, a visitor centre, picnic areas and nature trails. Guides to the reservoir have been specially written and amplified by maps. There is a recreation officer and rangers to show you the way and answer your questions. Good taste, imagination and respect for the countryside are all evident. Yet I find my admiration tempered with regret. This was a quiet valley. There was a gateway from which you could look over slopes, hedgerows, meadows and woods. It was not quite tame and yet not wild. There were no tourist attractions. I liked it best at dusk, when a few of the brightest stars began to shine through the branches. It was silent then.

Hawkhurst is a large and sprawling village in two parts, an older part called 'The Moor', which is the village green and looks rural, and a newer part called 'Highgate', which has a parade of shops and looks urban. Each has its own church. The Moor church is a handsome ragstone building of the fourteenth and fifteenth centuries. It was badly damaged in the war but was skilfully restored. It has a crenellated tower with a turret in the corner, like so many churches in the eastern part of the Weald. Highgate church was built in 1861 of sandstone; its spire is a prominent landmark.

One thing above all else brought notoriety to Hawkhurst. That was a gang of smugglers which operated from the village in the eighteenth century. The most powerful smuggling gang in the south-east, it was utterly ruthless, and any romantic notions about smuggling were soon banished by its brutality. Terror brought great riches to this gang, whose members even built warehouses in which to store goods waiting for transport to London. They also combined highway robbery with their smuggling enterprises. No law-abiding citizen dared voice the slightest criticism, still less opposition, for fear of reprisals. Magistrates convicted with reluctance and when they did, transport of the convicted by cart to Maidstone gaol was unguarded and rescue easy.

Deliverance eventually came in 1747 from the people of Goudhurst, who formed their own militia under a man called Sturt. The smugglers declared they would burn the village and kill all captives, and arrogantly stated the date and hour when they intended to do so. A strong force duly appeared at the appointed time, but unfortunately for them Sturt was an ex-soldier. Defences were skilfully organized. The smugglers walked into a trap. When they opened fire, the response from various well-chosen positions, including rooftops and the church tower, was instant, accurate and devastating. Four smugglers were killed and many wounded.

Others, taken alive, were tried and hanged.

Eastward, the country changes rapidly. The trees and the hills recede, the land slopes down to the Rother which begins to widen. Marsh pastures and the gleam of water become pronounced features of the landscape. We are back on the fringes of Romney Marsh, and in no time we find ourselves on the banks of the moat surrounding Bodiam Castle, one of the most visited of National Trust properties.

Bodiam Castle was built purely as a military installation, and not as part residence and part castle to be brought into action if an enemy threatened. It was built by Sir Edward Dalyngrigge in 1385 for the sole purpose of blocking marauding French if they should venture up the Rother Valley after pillaging Rye. The French never chanced their arm that far, but to this day Bodiam Castle looks what it was intended for, a fort. The Rother is still tidal as far as Bodiam Bridge, built in 1796; in the days of the French raiders it was also navigable.

The nearest the castle ever came to action was during the Wars of the Roses, in 1483, when the Lancastrians took it from the Yorkists, but apparently nobody was hurt. Despite its long history of non-violence, it seems likely that Cromwell 'slighted' the castle during the Civil War, and inside you will see signs of deliberate dismantlement. From then on it gradually fell into serious disrepair, from which sorry state it was rescued at the beginning of the nineteenth century by 'mad' Jack Fuller MP, of whom we shall learn more at Brightling. Lord Curzon bought it in 1917, thoroughly restored it and left it to the National Trust on his death in 1926. It is now regularly invaded every year by thousands of tourists. Green meadows lie serenely around it, reaching to hills south of the river, and to the countryside south of the Rother we now turn our attention.

The natural starting point from which to venture into this region is Heathfield. Probably about ninety out of every hundred people who say they know Heathfield are only half right. What they call Heathfield is a long, wide and rather pleasant street, lined with good, well-stocked shops on the A265. But there is another, old Heathfield, a mile and a half down a lane. This is the original Heathfield, now called Old Heathfield. The better-known Heathfield on the busy main road grew up round the

Polegate-Eridge railway line, completed in 1884, now closed.

You come upon Old Heathfield suddenly. It sits on the edge of a valley, a cluster of ancient cottages in quiet byways all leading to a prominent church and the Star Inn. Despite extensive nineteenth-century 'restorations', the church is still substantially thirteenth century, including the tower built of chalk with stone facing, and it replaced a pre-Norman church. There is no chalk nearer than the South Downs thirteen miles away, so how was it brought through the difficult forest? Much of the church was rebuilt in 1380 after damage by fire, and this rebuilding was the reason for the construction of the inn, almost in the shadow of the church. It was developed from a shelter provided for the men working on the church. There are big black beams inside, and a wide terrace outside overlooks the valley.

Heathfield has an enchanting legend. Every year on 4 April, traditional Heathfield fair day, an old lady releases a cuckoo from a basket, thus starting the season of spring. The old lady and the freed cuckoo are the motifs of the wrought-iron village sign.

Heathfield has satellites. Small clusters of cottages are grouped round the village, not in any sort of design but informally, as if they had grown there, almost but not quite independent of the village.

One of these 'little Heathfields' is called Cade Street, and its name has been linked with the fifteenth-century rebel who, as we have seen, had the backing of Maidstone in his fight against government policy in 1450. Alexander Iden, High Sheriff of Kent, is said to have killed Cade, and Shakespeare, in *Henry VI*, places the scene in Kent. The spot might have been Hothfield, but some historians argue strongly for Heathfield, and I dare say the argument will go on for a long time and may never be resolved. It is, however, certain that Cade Street was not named after the execution, if such it could be called, of Jack Cade. The name is an adulteration of Cat Street, which is derived from Katterstrete, cart street. Nevertheless, a stone monument to the rebel, whose real name might have been John Mortimer, has been erected on the roadside bank. It bears the inscription, 'Near this spot was slain the notorious rebel Jack Cade by Alexander Iden, Sheriff of Kent, AD 1450. His body was carried to London and his head fixed upon London Bridge. This is the success of all rebels, and this fortune chanceth ever to traitors.' The monument attracts tourists.

Heathfield Park, Heathfield's 'big house', was the home of General George Augustus Eliott, who successfully defended Gibraltar in the French-Spanish siege of 1779-83. He commanded five thousand soldiers and two thousand marines and sailors against besieging forces which at their peak numbered 33,000. The little garrison seemed doomed in 1782, when a formidable attack was mounted with 140 pieces of artillery which had to be transported across the Bay of Algeciras by night on ten gargantuan rafts. The attackers reckoned that the floating batteries would blast the fort out of existence, and they might well have been right had the guns got the chance to loose the projected barrage. With cool audacity Eliott attacked. But he did not go for the enemy's ranks. He concentrated on the rafts, which he subjected to an unrelenting hail of red-hot shot dubbed by his men 'roasted potatoes'. The strategy was an overwhelming triumph. Eight of the rafts were destroyed by fire. The glare lit up the face of the rock and enabled the Marines to rescue three hundred of the enemy from drowning. Eliott was created Lord Heathfield of Gibraltar in 1787, and he died three years later aged seventy-two. His successor to the Park, Francis Newberry, friend of the novelist Oliver Goldsmith, built a round tower in his memory. It is still there, inside the walls which surround the parkland and called, naturally, Gibraltar Tower.

Another redoubtable Englishman lived six miles east. He was small, diffident and shy, but of all the devoted servants of Empire he was the most famous. He was Rudyard Kipling, and his home was Bateman's, Burwash, from 1902 to 1936, when he died. Bateman's is a biggish house, and its sandstone walls and tall chimneys glow warmly in the sun. It was built for an ironmaster in 1604, and a little river called the Dudwell ambles through the grounds on its way to join the Rother. Kipling was inventive in more ways than with words. With the help of Sir William Willcocks, designer of the Aswan Dam on the River Nile, he harnessed the water-power in his garden to supply electric light. Bateman's was bequeathed to the National Trust in 1939 by Kipling's widow and, so far as possible, the Trust maintains it as it was when the Kipling family lived in it. The writer's study seems so much a lived-in and worked-in room that on the threshold you automatically pause to be greeted. Kipling called it his workshop, and he took considerable trouble to see that he could do his work in it with maximum convenience. Ink, pens, paper are all ready to hand on a broad seventeenth-century chestnut table. Two big globes of the world and an outsize wastepaper basket stand nearby, and the walls are lined from top to bottom with books. The table would have been too high for Kipling, so he had blocks fitted upon the club feet of his eighteenth-century chair, raising it to the exact height he stipulated. This enabled him to sit in comfort. Over his work and over the table he looked out through a wide window and up a long green valley he grew to love deeply.

There was a watermill in the garden beside the river, and Kipling introduces it to you in *Puck of Pook's Hill*:

See you our little mill that clacks
So busy by the brook?
She has ground her corn and paid her tax
Ever since Domesday Book.

The Trust has restored the mill. It now grinds wheat into flour for sale in the nearby Trust shop.

Kipling designed the gardens, and visitors find in them not only colour but also restfulness, and are thereby reminded that

the glory of the garden
lies in more than meets the eye.

In Burwash village they speak of Kipling not only with respect but also with affection; they have not gone 'Kiplingesque', which he would have loathed. The village is built along the high southern lip of the Rother Valley, and views across the multi-coloured countryside are superb. These are pleasant brick sidewalks shaded by pollarded limes and raised well above the road, and here and there partly overhung by gables of ancient houses. At the top of the village, where the road takes a sharp turning to the left and also a sudden dip, you find the church among trees, some of it early Norman, some twelfth and thirteenth century. An iron grave slab has been placed against a wall inside. It was cast in the fourteenth century, probably the earliest example in existence of a grave slab of Wealden iron. It bears the inscription 'Orate P. Annema Jhone

Collins.' Only 'P. Annema' can be clearly read, so the children in Kipling's *Rewards and Fairies* called that part of the church 'Panama Corner'.

Another poet of Burwash, the Reverend James Hurdis, curate there from 1785 to 1791, did not see the tranquil countryside that Kipling saw. He lived among the iron foundries which he describes in a long poem, *The Village Curate*:

> ... the heavy wheel moves round,
> And ever and again lets fall the loud
> And awful hammer, that compounds the ear,
> And makes the firm earth shake.

Burwash Forge was one of the longest-lived in the Weald. It was still in operation at the end of the eighteenth century. The Romans may have worked it.

South of Burwash you enter a complex of lanes more puzzling even than those which so upset E.V. Lucas. You are practically certain to lose your way, but don't worry: you won't actually get lost, and the quiet solitude of this countryside is something to savour. The lanes turn this way and that, up hill and down, through plantations of sweet chestnut, through mixed woodlands and by little sloping meadows. Sometimes a lane twists upwards but suddenly changes its mind and twists down instead, and you feel that a hilltop somewhere has somehow eluded you. Every so often you catch a glimpse of a tall obelisk, and so long as you draw gradually nearer to it, you are on course, for this is your objective. When you reach it, you have climbed one of the highest points in the High Weald, Brightling Down, 646 feet above sea-level, with vast views in every direction. It is not a down in the accepted sense, it is nowhere near either the North or the South Downs, it has no chalk in its make-up and no sweeping curves so characteristic of true downland. But you do enjoy a unique distant view of the South Downs. You see their eastern end head on, a five-mile wall from Beachy Head northward to Combe Hill, and then a long line stretching away at an angle as far as the eye can see to the north-west, silver grey and rising abruptly from the blue Weald immediately below. The confusing 'Down' is from the Saxon *'dun'*, a hill.

The tall stone obelisk is a folly, one of a number of follies in the district built by 'Mad' Jack Fuller. It looks like Cleopatra's Needle and is called the Brightling Needle. Two more follies stand within a short distance, one an observatory, now a private house, for Fuller was a keen astronomer, and the other a complete mystery until you find out about it. It is a carefully shaped stone cone. Fuller told his friends that the spire of Dallington church could be seen from his grounds. He was proved wrong. So he built a 'spire' where he felt the Dallington spire should have been in the view from his home. It is certainly convincing from the distance and always bewilders visitors, who carefully note the spire but can never find the church. A fourth folly is impressive and unlike the others. Fuller built it for a specific and practical purpose, his own interment. It is a tomb shaped like a small pyramid in the churchyard, next to his home, Rose Hill, now Brightling Park.

Fuller died in 1834, aged seventy-seven, twenty-four years after the completion of his tomb. He was a man of stark contrasts. He provided work for many local people but he was also deeply involved in slave trading. He was a Member of Parliament from 1801 to 1812 but had scant respect for parliamentary procedure and once referred to the Speaker as an 'insignificant little fellow in a wig', for which he was carried from the House. We have already noted his care for the historic through his rescue of Bodiam Castle. Pitt recognized his talent and abilities and offered him a peerage, but Fuller brusquely turned down the offer with, 'I was born Jack Fuller and Jack Fuller I'll die.'

Brightling village is an old and secret little place among the trees. The name comes from the Saxon Byrhtlingan Beorhthelm's or Beorhtel's people. Domesday Book called it Brislinga. The Saxons built a church there. The Normans supplanted it with a new building soon after they arrived. This building has been added to and modified through the centuries, and today's church is a solid-looking, sandstone structure with a sturdy tower just topping the nearby cottages.

Unlike Brightling, Dallington, two miles off, is compact. Cottages cluster close together, and the different types and sizes of roofs make an intriguing silhouette which changes its pattern as you move about. The church looks un-English but certainly is not. The sixteenth-century tower supports a short stone spire, an unusual feature in the Weald. Nothing could look more English than the manor house next door, an ancient and unspoilt building rich in dark oak timbers.

It is now a straightforward matter to travel on to Battle.

There is a terrace on a hill overlooking green pastures and stately trees. It is a tranquil scene and not at all uncommon in the south of England. But this is unique ground, and thousands of people in the course of the year stand upon the terrace and contemplate the sloping pastures, silently. For where they stand on the terrace, and down there in the meadows, the course of English history was changed in a day. This is the site of the Battle of Hastings in 1066, when the Norman William and the Saxon Harold fought for the English throne. The place was called Senlac.

With the help of American money the whole area became a national possession in 1976, and it attracted 120,000 visitors within a year.

William's forces were encamped six miles away, at Hastings, and from Hastings they marched to battle at dawn on 14 October. Harold and his army had just marched over two hundred miles from the north of England, where they had defeated a force of Norwegians. They were weary but they might well have won. All day the battle raged. Hour after hour death came by the axe and the club, by the sword and the lance, and, from the Norman archers, by thick showers of arrows. Harold's forces had the better position on the hill, and the Normans had never met such stubborn opposition. But William's men were better disciplined, and that was what counted in the end. At dusk a section of the Norman army feigned flight, an ancient ruse which should have deceived nobody. The house carls around Harold kept their ranks, but to a section of less trained soldiers, weary but scenting victory at last, the temptation was too great. They gave chase and were cut to pieces. The Normans thereby achieved superiority, and man by man the stubborn English fell. There came the moment just before darkness when King Harold, too, met death, probably not by the legendary arrow but much more likely by axe or sword.

William vowed that if he won, 'Upon this place of battle I will found a suitable free monastery for the salvation of you all, and specially for those who fall.'

He was as good as his word.

Crowds of craftsmen and other workmen built their rough quarters round the site of the great battle. These early, rough habitations gradually gave way to more substantial buildings which developed into a pleasant town close by the abbey and, almost by natural process, from 'this place of battle', took its name: Battle.

The altar was placed over the spot where Harold died. You will find it in the ruins of the abbey church, which at first was not particularly large but was probably beautiful. The first monastic buildings were also modest. But the monastery expanded and the church was very much enlarged. The abbey eventually became a place of great spiritual and political influence, of architectural grandeur, of agricultural progress, and a noted centre of learning.

King Henry VIII put a stop to all that with his Dissolution of the Monasteries Act of 1536.

On 27 May 1538 the King's Commissioners, Sir John Gage and Richard Layton, rode into Battle with their servants, demanded admission to the abbey and duly reported on their findings. The result was a foregone conclusion: the abbey was doomed. The great abbey church was reduced to heaps of rubble and most of the other buildings ruined. The abbot's house, splendid gatehouse, dorter, frater and kitchen were left. Next year the King gave the entire site to Sir Anthony Browne, his chief of horse, who occupied the house and planted a garden where the abbey church had stood.

A dispossessed, irate but intrepid monk, preferring an eye for an eye to turning the other cheek, is said to have faced up to Sir Anthony and called down upon him this curse: 'By fire and water thy line shall perish.' Sir Anthony's line perished exactly like that, but 250 years later, as we shall see when we get to Midhurst.

The gatehouse, built in 1338, is well preserved and gives you some idea of what the rest of the abbey looked like. It is the most striking building not only on the abbey site but also in the whole town of Battle.

Within a few yards of the gatehouse a timber-framed house catches everybody's eye. It was built about 1420 and may have replaced an earlier building. It is called the Pilgrim's Rest and, as its name suggests, it was a rest house for pilgrims visiting the abbey. It is now a restaurant.

Battle's parish church is often mistakenly thought to be part of the abbey, which it almost was. At first, the inhabitants of the little town were allowed to worship in the abbey church, but this led to inconveniences as the town grew. It also infringed Benedictine rules, and Battle was a Benedictine abbey. So the monks built a church nearby to serve the parishioners under the direction of the abbot. That was about 1115. A few fragments survive of this early church which has grown steadily through the centuries. It is now a large structure, mostly of the thirteenth century with additions during the two succeeding centuries, including a conspicuous fifteenth-century tower.

Most of the buildings in Battle today are fifteenth to eighteenth century with much timber framing, hanging tiles and brick and stone; and there are scarcely two rooftops of the same height. Stonework from the abbey ruins is easily recognizable.

A straight run up the A2100 for about five miles brings you to Robertsbridge, climbing the south bank of the Rother and therefore sometimes said to be an adulteration of Rotherbridge. But the name is more likely to have derived from Robert de St Martin, who may have founded the Cistercian abbey a little less than a mile down the river, now a ruin and part of a farm.

The village bestrides the A21 to Hastings and in the summer is noisy with traffic but a pleasant place in other seasons. Houses stand close together along the main street in an amicable jostle, with fine examples of sixteenth-century and seventeenth-century architecture. Pretty corners greet you the minute you step off the main street, a quiet patio or an outside stairway, with a skyline of steep, red rooftops which you can look at with pleasure, forgetting time. Robertsbridge had a cattle market whose origins could be traced back to 1253. It was transferred to Battle in 1954.

Today a flourishing country industry keeps the name of the village to the foremost wherever in the world they play cricket, for on the outskirts, among woodland, craftsmen make cricket bats. The enterprise was established almost accidentaly about 1870 by a local cricket enthusiast, Mr L.J. Nicolls, who made bats for his cricketing friends and then found himself faced with such a demand that he was forced to go commercial. The bats quickly gained renown, and the famous Dr W.G. Grace selected them for all important matches. He scored his hundredth century with a Nicolls bat and with the same bat knocked up a thousand runs one May.

Over the bridge, Salehurst is grouped in a homely way about a church begun in the early fourteenth century. It has steadily grown ever since, but the many architectural styles do not jar, not even the Victorian contributions. This is also the church for Robertsbridge, which has none of its own.

Eastward the land becomes increasingly remote, though never wild. Pasture and woodland predominate, with here and there a modest stretch of arable, here and there an orchard. The influence of the widening Rother grows stronger, and the views from hilltops become more extensive. Villages sometimes snuggle in the valleys, sometimes crown the hills. They have not attracted the speculative developers, so there is no red rash of 'desirable residences', all depressingly identical. They have grown up with the surrounding rural crafts, the chief of which are farming and forestry.

Staple Cross, standing back from the valley, is centred on a small square where four roads once met. When tarmac came, one of the roads was left untreated and is now a pleasant track to Robertsbridge.

Ewhurst, high up on the edge of the valley, commands a view both wide and lovely; nothing mars it. John Wesley, riding through on missionary work, stayed here at the invitation of the Anglican curate, the Reverend John Richardson, in a sixteenth-century house of black beams and white plaster. Richardson became a great friend and follower of Wesley and read the service at his funeral at London's City Road Chapel in 1791. At his own death Richardson was buried in Wesley's vault in the chapel. The house is still called the Preacher's House.

The twelfth- and thirteenth-century sandstone church, mercifully unrestored, had a high, shingled spire with a kind of kink in it, due to an unexplained change of pitch while building was in progress. Such small mysteries bring added interest to the traveller. What could have caused the miscalculation, if miscalculation there were?

The most striking feature of Ewhurst is not, however, the church spire but a group of oasthouses whose cones, rising dramatically against the sky, are a landmark from long distances up and down the valley. In the early 1950s they were converted into private homes and are now set off by bright gardens and blessed by that far-reaching Rother Valley view.

The one large village in the area is Northiam. Its heart is a large green, and when you arrive there you momentarily feel you have been transported back to the low Wealden plain in Kent, for Northiam is a village of white weatherboarded houses. They surround the green, sometimes in clusters, sometimes standing alone, and they spill over to the lanes that lead down to the valley and into the pastoral and wooded countryside. Domesday calls it Hiham (high land), and this evolved into North Hiam. The green is liberally planted with trees, and in the shelter of an oak on this green Queen Elizabeth I is said to have eaten her mid-day meal on her way to Rye on 11 August 1573. A gnarled and venerable oak on the north-west side of the green is considered to be the tree thus honoured.

The white weatherboards are relieved here and there by black timber-framed walls with white plaster fill-ins, and you even find houses which are part timber-framed and part white weatherboards; they do not look peculiar or out of place. The most outstanding of the timber-framed houses is Great Dixter, whose close perpendicular black beams support a red tiled roof with tall chimneys. It has endured since the fifteenth century, with some skilful help from Sir Edwin Lutyens in 1910. The gardens are nationally known and are open to the public in spring, summer and autumn. But the greatest contrast in the white village is the dark brown and grey sandstone church, whose tower is embellished by both turret and a stone spire. Saxon masons probably built a church here under Norman direction fifty to a hundred years after the invasion. This early work can be seen in the lower part of the tower and the west wall. The rest was replaced by fourteenth and fifteenth-century work. Then the church remained untouched until 1834, when architect Sydney Smirke enlarged it. The spire and octagonal turret were positioned on the tower in the late sixteenth century, and the spire was raised ten feet in 1860.

You go on through woodland and pasture, through valleys and over hills, and presently you come to Beckley, a big village arranged as one group with a number of smaller attendant groups around. It is a remote corner, unspoiled, very green, very leafy and quiet. Beckley church stands a little apart from the village, down a lane. Its shingled spire rises from a tower begun in the eleventh century and finished in the twelfth, and inside there is a parish chest carved out of a single tree trunk bearing early ironwork. Beckley was another important iron-working centre, and Beckley Furnace, now a farmstead, operated until the end of the eighteenth century. There are two exquisite timber-framed houses nearby, both early sixteenth century, Great Horsepen, which was an inn, and Little Horsepen, where the ostler slept.

The valley now widens to the Rother Levels below Peasmarsh, and at Iden you are on a sort of tableland opposite the Isle of Oxney and above the green expanses of Romney Marsh.

Now we turn south to the Brede Levels and three conspicuous villages. Sedlescombe is grouped round a sloping green with wellhouse and pump (dated 1900) in the middle. The famous centre for refugee children, Pestalozzi Village, is about a mile away. In the thirteenth-century church at Brede, about three miles east, there is an arresting statue of the Virgin and Child which the sculptor Clare Sheridan carved from a tree grown at Brede Place. The view from the churchyard across the Levels is magnificent, and at Udimore you are once again on the fringe of the Marsh, though also high above it. Rye is about $3\frac{1}{2}$ miles down the road, and on the other side of Brede Levels you come suddenly to the end of the High Weald, which falls abruptly into the sea in a cascade of tawny cliffs, gorse and bracken. The name of this dramatic region, the Fire Hills, does not, however, have anything to do with the colour of the sandstone cliffs, or with beacons or any other kind of fire. It is derived from the blaze of flowering gorse in spring which, on the high cliffs, can be seen far out to sea. So can the tower of Fairlight church, a familiar landmark for sailors. On a clear day the coast of France stands boldly up from the hard horizon of the sea.

There are about four miles of these cliffs, with Hastings at the western end and Fairlight Cove in the east. Hastings is a major seaside resort and is not truly part of the Weald. It was a Saxon port called Haestingas after Haesta or Haesten, chief of the tribe Haestingas, and at that time forest and swamps pressed hard upon its landward sides. As we have seen, it was from Hastings that Duke William launched his invasion, finding a reasonably negotiable ridge along which his troops could march to Senlac. He built a timber castle on the Hastings clifftop, and three years later his followers replaced it with a stone castle, of which considerable fragments remain. Like all the other Cinque ports, Hastings suffered great damage from the savage storms of the thirteenth century, which entirely destroyed the harbour and half the castle.

St Leonards and Bexhill, the two close neighbours of Hastings, are also alien to the Weald, though pleasant resorts in themselves. But reaching westward from Bexhill are big stretches of flat marsh pasture considered to be among the most important wetlands of Europe. These marshlands are the Pevensey Levels.

6

Pevensey

Farmhouses, trees, farm buildings, belts of reeds and sheep and cattle, stand out above the flat pastures of Pevensey Levels even more sharply than they do on Romney Marsh, particularly at evening. Then the sharp light of sunset invests them with drama. It is a place of silhouettes, and the most splendid and the most dramatic is the Roman-Norman castle. The rugged ruins of the Roman walls and the Norman keep sharply break the skyline, and the steep roofs of the village below stand out in a stark and serried pattern above the pastures. It is an uncompromising pattern, almost aloof, yet the village itself, when you are in it, does not strike you as angular or bleak. Far from it. It is a comfortable, compact and rather cosy village. The low-hung houses sit close upon the level land, snuggling together, successfully defying the bitter winter winds that sweep over the marshes from the east. Rooms are warm and gardens are sheltered. Crocuses come early at Pevensey, and summer lingers far into autumn. It is a friendly and a welcoming place, in marked contrast to the strife and violence that so frequently engulfed it in its long history. A busy road passes through the entire length of the village, but the road is narrow, winding and closely flanked by the houses, so that traffic is slowed and more muted than you might suppose.

Pevensey is a highlight in all history books. It was important both politically and commercially, and it owed its status to the sea, which almost washed its doorstep. The Romans established it. With them it was simply a case of security and nothing else. Few places could have been more dreary, desolate or inhospitable. But its strategic position was exactly what the Romans wanted. There was a shallow hill at the end of a lonely promontory, and upon it the Roman engineers built a fortress of exceptional strength to form a link in a chain of defences along the coast from Porchester, near Portsmouth, to Brancaster in Norfolk. There were ten of these

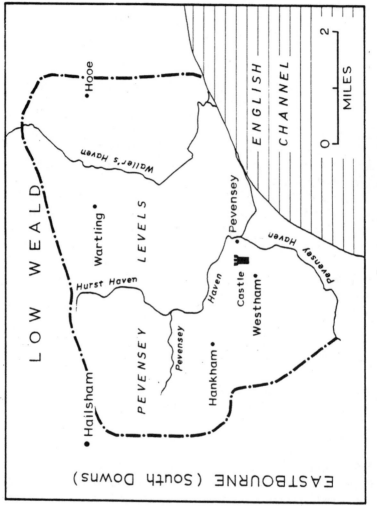

Pevensey

fortresses, possibly eleven, and we have already seen the ruins of one at Lemanis, but the ruins at Pevensey are vastly more impressive and better preserved.

Historians have assumed that the purpose of the forts was to repel Saxon pirates, who were becoming an increasing nuisance, and therefore this particular stretch of coast is called the Saxon Shore. But a tentative query has been raised about the reason for setting up such defences. The Saxon marauders of that time could not possibly breach, climb over or in any other way subdue the walls of those formidable forts, and certainly not the walls at Pevensey, which the Romans called Anderida. Here they were twelve feet thick of flint and sandstone rubble faced with sandstone and ironstone, with binding courses of red brick. They were twenty feet to twenty-five feet high and some still are after seventeen hundred years. They enclosed an area of about ten acres. In this fortified enclosure wooden military huts were arranged with Roman precision, and the garrison was always ready for instant action. There were only two entrances, one westward and opening to land, the other east, overlooking a long and sheltered estuary whose waters lapped the walls and opened southward to the sea. This estuary provided a first-class harbour and base for warships. Similar military and naval defences were established at all the other coastal forts, and it has been suggested that to build up such massive war power against unskilled pirates was unlikely to say the least.

If not the Saxon marauders, who then? Upon the scene appears a shadowy figure called Carausius, who in his day was anything but shadowy. He was a brilliant sailor and achieved high rank in the Roman fleet guarding the sea lanes between Gaul and Britain. In 286 he revolted against Emperor Maximian and proclaimed himself Emperor, and it seems his forces backed him. It was Carausius who built the forts on the Saxon Shore, no doubt with the professed intention of keeping out the Teuton hordes at all costs, but it is a strong possibility that he also intended to use them as bases from which to repel any forces Maximian might despatch to destroy him. He knew this would happen, and when it did he won, almost certainly through superior naval skill. Official Roman historians blamed the weather. Carausius ruled Britain for seven years; then, in 293, following a regrettable Roman tradition, he was murdered. In 296 the province was re-conquered without much difficulty.

For whatever purpose the forts were built, they were eventually used to the utmost. Rome weakened. The Empire constricted before the attacks of skilled armies on far-off frontiers. The Legions were gradually withdrawn, the defences left in the hands of Romanized Celts, and as Britain grew more vulnerable, so the barbarians increased their pressure. Presently, the Legions all gone, Britain lay defenceless. Then the Saxons came in hordes, not as raiders for a day but as determined invaders. The forts of the Saxon Shore were overrun and in 491, according to the *Anglo-Saxon Chronicle*, Saxon invaders fell upon Anderida and massacred every Briton in the place. That forlorn episode closed the history of Anderida for six centuries. Even its name disappeared. People called the spot Pefenesea, which could have meant Pefen's river, or possibly Pefen's island. Pefen was probably an obscure Saxon chieftain, but he nevertheless gave his name to a town which became a byword. But not for many generations.

The darkness that fell upon Anderida did not lift until that memorable day, 28 September 1066, when William the Norman arrived off Pevensey with a fleet of nearly seven hundred ships and ten thousand men. That, however, was not according to his carefully drawn-up invasion strategy, which was to land at Haestingas. The capricious sea between England and France was in a bad mood, and the fleet was forced westward far off course. Worse was to come. Walking up the beach, William stumbled, to the dismay of his men, who thought this second setback a bad omen, foretelling probabaly defeat. But not William. 'Don't worry,' he cried, grabbing a handful of shingle. 'Look! Already I've seized my kingdom.' Or words to that effect. Then they all went on to Hastings, and after that northward to beat Harold at Senlac, now called Battle, as we have seen. That landing at Pevensey was the last successful invasion of Britain.

The Normans, great castle-builders themselves, instantly recognized first-class defence work. They gazed with considerably respect at Pevensey Castle, in very good condition even after all those centuries of British weather. They did not pull it down and rebuild it and, unlike the Saxons, they did not ignore it, leaving it quietly to moulder and fall apart. They skilfully restored it, and in the south-east corner they built a keep which is still the most prominent part of the fortress.

William gave Pevensey to his half-brother Robert of Mortain, who founded a small borough almost within the shadows of the castle. It quickly became an important port and the ancestor of the Pevensey you see today. The borough joined the Cinque Ports Confederation in the early thirteenth century as a 'limb' of Hastings, and the borough seal of Pevensey is the oldest possessed by any of these ports.

With the Normans, Pevensey entered a period of intrigue and strife. Probably no other castle in Britain has endured such turbulence. It began only twenty-two years after William's arrival. In 1088 William 'Rufus', son of the Conqueror, laid siege against Robert of Mortain's brother, Bishop Odo, who was holding the castle for William's elder brother, Robert, Duke of Normandy. Rufus won. The list of squabbles which succeeded one another reads like an inventory. The most famous came in 1264, when the supporters of Henry III took refuge in the castle after their defeat by Simon de Montfort at the Battle of Lewes. Though de Montfort laid siege, he could neither starve out the refugees nor assault the castle. He had to withdraw. James I, King of the Scots, was held prisoner at Pevensey in 1406. Numberless refugees pinned their hopes on Pevensey for a passage from these shores and safety from their enemies.

Disputes and clashes continued unabated for centuries, and in the end they were stopped not by anybody's military superiority but by the quiet processes of nature. The sea silted up, and after the defeat of the Spanish Armada the fort was considered useless as a defence. The tumult and the shouting died. The clamour of the centuries receded with the sea. Quiet rural charm took over, and the redoubtable old walls were left to crumble and decay.

But their service was not yet done. Secret gun emplacements were built into the walls in 1940, and the guns faced out to sea, the way the Saxons came. But the Nazis did not come. Today these artillery positions have become a point of pilgrimage for visitors, who do not look immediately out to sea, however, for wide marsh pastures now lie where the waves washed, sheep and cattle graze where ships sailed and the sea is more than a mile away.

Pevensey Castle is now as tranquil a place as you are likely to find. Children play in perfect safety on the grass, a ten-acre oasis free of all traffic. Swallows and martins skim through the summer air between the walls upon which small flowers grow.

When you walk down the long street from the castle's east gate, you are bound to notice a prominent building on your left. This is the Old Mint House. Pevensey was granted the privilege of its own mint, and this was briefly mentioned in Domesday Book. Pevensey-minted coins from the reigns of King William I (the Conqueror), William 'Rufus' and Stephen are now exhibited at the British Museum. It is claimed that the Old Mint House stands on the site of the original mint house. It dates from about 1432 but was considerably altered in the sixteenth century. It contains twenty-eight rooms and much massive medieval timber work, panelling and carving. Andrew Borde, or Boorde ('Merry Andrew'), sixteenth-century physician, author, traveller and wit, lived in the Old Mint House, and his brother, Dr Richard Borde, was vicar of Pevensey and Westham from 1529 to 1541.

An equally arresting but very different building stands further down the street. It is a little, square construction with a distinctly Spanish look. In fact, there is nothing Spanish about it whatever. It is entirely English and very Pevensey. It is the old court house and town hall, and it is probably the smallest of either in the country. It dates from the sixteenth century and is a gabled building of two storeys. An exterior staircase takes you to the upper floor, which was the court room and council chamber. The lower storey was a lock-up of two cells. Anybody found guilty of a capital offence was dealt with there and then and practically on the spot. He was taken down the street and thrown off a bridge into a wide stretch of water called Pevensey Haven, where he drowned. 'Haven' here does not mean a sheltered inlet on the coast; it is a stretch of moving water, usually slow, drained from the land. There are several such havens on the Levels.

Pevensey was a hotbed of smuggling in the eighteenth century. It was an easy matter to bring contraband goods into the town from the sea, and hide them until it seemed safe to transport them over the next stage of a carefully planned journey to London. The church was a principal hiding-place. Unfortunately for the smugglers, a strong force of Excisemen was stationed at Pevensey, and ferocious battles were fought between the 'free traders' and the Preventive men, whose headquarters stood handily only a few yards from the Court House. These buildings are still there, now two private houses with meticulous pebble facing, mullioned window frames and fine masonry round a doorway.

The sandstone, pebble and flint church built about 1270 replaced an earlier Norman building which was badly damaged, with much of the town, during de Montfort's unsuccessful assault on the castle after the Battle of Lewes. It stands back from a narrow lane where you are as likely to meet a horse as a car. Its tower is surmounted by a modest spire of oak shingles, and it makes a tranquil picture among sheltering trees with the level pastures beyond. It looks smallish from the lane but the interior is surprisingly large. Extensive restoration were carried out in 1879.

The castle and castle grounds separate Pevensey from the village of Westham. Nevertheless, it is hard to realize that these are two villages, for you do not notice when you leave one and enter the other. Westham church, just outside the castle west gate, was built by the Normans soon after their arrival. It was extensively enlarged about 1300, when a massive west tower was added. The walls of both tower and main body of the church are all of flint and stone; they convey an impression of great strength, and at first glance you might think they were part of the castle.

Pevensey Levels look like Romney Marsh on a smaller scale until you look more closely. Then you discover major differences. The Marsh has been almost wholly tamed. The Levels remain half tamed and partly wild. That state is essential for the wildlife of the region. Agriculture is practised on a restrained scale and is not highly intensive. In the 'seventies and early 'eighties it seemed almost certain that intensive arable farming was going to displace the rough pasture farming of centuries. Major drainage schemes involving powerful pumps would have raised or lowered the water-table at will, making possible the use of big ploughs and other cultivation equipment. But conservationists stepped in.

There are eleven thousand acres of the Levels, and upon the entire area the Nature Conservancy Council placed a protective designation, Site of Special Scientific Interest. The Nature Conservancy Council is the Government body which promotes nature conservation in Britain. The SSSI designations were created in 1949 and were given increased strength under the Wildlife and

Countryside Act 1981. Farmers and landowners may not change land use in an area which has been covered by the SSSI designation without first consulting the Council. If the Council disagrees with the proposed change, it could offer alternatives such as a reasonable management agreement. It has repeatedly emphasized that farmers should be compensated for loss of income or for actual expenditure resulting from managing their land in a way which would make conservation possible and encourage the wildlife of the region.

Drainage is no new thing on Pevensey Levels. The Romans made no attempt at it, though they were well qualified to do so, as their work on Romney Marsh demonstrates. The Saxons cut a few experimental ditches in the brackish wilderness which extended northwards from the town. Further modest drainage operations were carried out through the centuries, practically all of them individual efforts to suit this or that farmer's needs, and without any concerted plan. The result is many miles of reed-fringed and slow-moving water which has had little if any effect on the shallow pools and reed beds dotted about the rough marsh pastures. A delicate balance developed between man and nature, which has led to the evolution of a magnificent habitat for a great variety of wildlife, particularly wildfowl, water plants, and a teeming life in the not quite static water. That is the state of Pevensey Levels today. The rugged ruins of the fortress overlook a low, green and tawny land, criss-crossed by streams, ditches and dykes and it is vital that the present balance between wildlife and marsh grazing by cattle and sheep should be maintained. In their semi-wild state the Levels provide much more than a subsistence living for the farmers but not what they might have expected from the more intensive type of agriculture which a sophisticated drainage scheme would have made possible. But that would have pushed an abundant wildlife to the brink of extinction.

More than fifty-two species of birds breed on the Levels, including redshank, snipe and yellow wagtails, and for these birds the area is a vital habitat. If they were ever forced away from the Levels, it is unlikely that they would find alternative homes. Great numbers of additional wildfowl fly down to the Levels in winter, among them wigeon, mallard, teal, snipe and golden plover and around ten thousand lapwings (peewits). Cold weather brings geese, especially whitefronts, and whooper and Bewick's swans, which join the resident mute swans, the largest of our swans and by no means mute.

Winter is my favourite time for visiting the Levels. There is water and wetness everywhere. Giant white willows stand with their feet in pools and runnels and their uppermost twigs high in the air. Water slithers across the narrow lanes and lies in invisible shallow lakes just beneath the tussocks and grass. Those unwise enough not to wear waterproof boots are apt to discover these concealed lakes with great discomfort. The birds revel in it, frequently heard but not seen. As you carefully step from tussock to tussock, a snipe will suddenly explode upward from your feet, rocketing wildly into the pale blue sky until you lose sight of it in a faint haze which you had not realized was there. In times of bitter frost and snow the birds congregate along the water-courses, for there, if anywhere, they will find soft earth and consequently food.

Not only birds flock to the Levels in winter. There are also bird-watchers. They are of all ages, and it is encouraging to see so many young people with so keen an interest. They arrive on foot, on bicycles and on shaggy ponies, and around their necks dangle binoculars which would do credit to Ascot.

Some of the plants which grow along the waterways are both beautiful and rare, and one, the flowering rush, is spectacular. It grows up to four feet high and bears large umbels of inch-wide bright pink flowers in July and August. The pale lilac water-violet blooms from May to July. The pure white blooms, about $1\frac{1}{2}$ inches wide, of an extraordinary plant called the water-soldier appear from June to August. Until then the plant lives entirely under water. It never produces fruit.

Without the co-operation of farmers the prolific and varied wealth of natural life on the Levels would disappear as surely as it would under modern intensive agriculture. Despite the guidance of the Nature Conservancy Council, the Sussex Trust for Nature Conservation and the Farming and Wildlife Advisory Group, far too many well-intentioned but ill-informed conservationists believe that such marshland areas should be left alone. If human management were removed, the Levels would soon revert to a state which the Romans would recognize; when the soldiers looked north from their fortress they saw an impassable quagmire. It would offer habitats for much wildlife but they would be minimal compared with the vast abundance of refuges which wildlife finds today, and they would be infinitely less varied.

We have noted that winter is the best time for birds if you are looking for numbers and variety, but spring and summer, particularly early summer, have their advantages too, for these are the breeding seasons. At this time farm poultry often joins, temporarily, the unrestricted surge of life out on the marsh. On a warm, sunny morning in June I sat quietly on a bank and watched a goose lead her goslings up a sunken and narrow waterway overhung by reeds and tall grasses. I knew she would eventually take them back, but for a while she and her goslings were as wild as the mute swans nearby. You need to exercise a lot of patience if you are going to see the wild parade before you like this, but it is no hardship to sit on a warm bank in the sun with the fragrant scent of newly-turned hay within a few yards.

In addition to Pevensey village and Westham, there are two other, much smaller villages out on the Levels, Hooe and Wartling. Both stand on small hills about a mile and a half from each other, once they were probably little islands in the bog. Hooe is compact except for its chiefly fifteenth-century church down a long lane. It has a font of Sussex marble. Wartling church is partly thirteenth century, and its lectern departs from the traditional eagle with widespread wings. Here the Bible rests upon the wings of a heron, much more appropriate in such a region.

From this slightly east of centre part of the Levels you look over a great expanse of grass marshland, giving on to the Low Weald from which the South Downs rise abruptly; and it is to the Low Weald that we now turn.

7

The Low Weald

You feel rather than see an abrupt change in the landscape when you step off the Pevensey Levels. You are not much higher, a matter of a few feet, for there are no vestigial cliffs here as there are round Romney Marsh. You are still among pastures but the grass is different. It is cultivated and carefully tended, and hay and silage will be made from it. You are aware that there are no concealed pools beneath your feet. There are a few more trees, but it is not numbers that you notice: the trees are different. In place of willows there are oaks. There are more flowers in more gardens, and the birds are the birds which live near the habitations of man: the blackbirds and thrushes, the sparrows, robins and finches. You are in a more homely atmosphere. The wild is left behind. You are on the Low Weald, the belt of clay, occasionally veined with sandy loam, that lies immediately under the South Downs.

You come first to Herstmonceux, distinguished by its unusual castle, an ancient church and a thriving rural industry.

You go two miles down a winding tree-lined lane to castle and church, passing a hamlet called Flowers Green, which is as pretty as its name suggests. The castle might have been transported from a fairy-tale book. It has battlements and turrets, it is surrounded by a moat and it has a fine, open space in front, but it is not grim and it does not repel. It is a light and airy place, more country house than castle. It was, in fact, built more for comfort than combat, and it has never seen a fight since it was constructed in 1440. In one respect it is quite unlike most other castles, for it is built of brick. On a sunny summer evening the soft red of the walls, the green grass and the darker green trees mingle serenely together. The castle was dismantled in 1777 and remained a ruin until 1913, when it was restored, to be followed by a more thorough restoration in 1933.

The Admiralty bought the castle in 1946 for the Royal

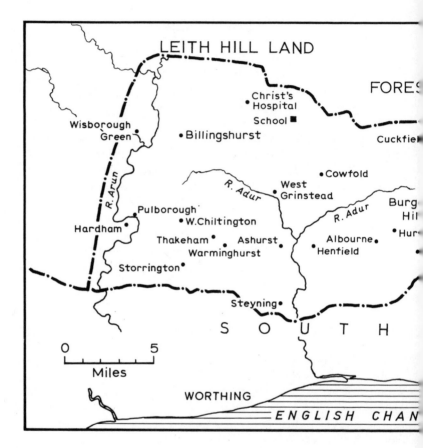

The Low Weald

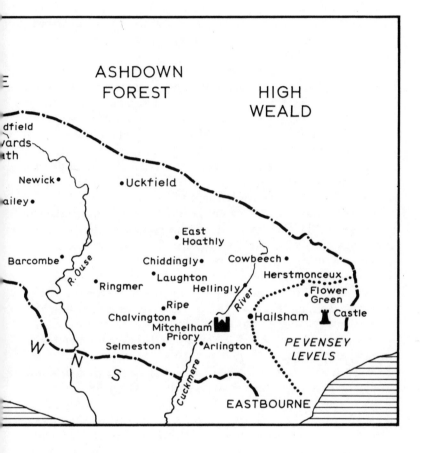

Greenwich Observatory to gain atmospheric clarity. In 1983 the main telescope was transferred to La Palma, the most westerly of the Canary Islands, where there is even more clarity and a lot less of what scientists call 'optical turbulence'. But Herstmonceux remains the base, and between Easter and the end of September visitors can still see the equipment which makes modern astronomy possible.

The Normans built the church, on the other side of the lane, about 1180, replacing a Saxon building, about which Domesday Book says succinctly, 'There is a church.' Nothing remains of this early church, which was probably of timber, but a good deal of the Norman building is still there. Most of the church, however, is fourteenth and fifteenth century.

The lane goes on a little further from church and castle to a farm. Then your eyes suddenly meet the grey-green expanse of the Levels, with a silver band of sea beyond.

The rural industry produces trugs. Trugs as we know them were invented by Mr Thomas Smith in a workshop in Herstmonceux about the middle of the last century. The Herstmonceux trug replaced a heavy, boat-like receptable, and demand for it by gardeners and horticultural enterprises has never slackened. It is still handmade from willow slats set in an ash or chestnut frame, and it is so strong that up-ended it will easily bear your weight if you sit on it, though that is not recommended. Garden-enthusiast Queen Victoria recognized its merits and ordered a number to made specially made for her.

The countryside round Herstmonceux is largely orchards, and in spring at blossom time it seems as if a little of the Garden of England has strayed there. Quiet byways thread through the orchards, often between high hedges, very necessary windbreaks; and lanes carry you onward out of the fruit-tree area. Such byways are as much a characteristic of the Low Weald as they are of the High Weald, lacking only the hills. They twist and turn between hedges, through woods and beside fields and meadows, and you can go from one end of this low landscape to the other by means of these narrow ways. You are not obliged to. You can drive along main roads at speed if you prefer, but you miss the spirit of the countryside if you do. Also, many of the most attractive villages are set deep among the farmlands and woods. They are closely tied

Bateman's, Burwash, home of Rudyard
Kipling. It was built by an ironmaster in 1604

The Pantiles, Tunbridge Wells

Cranbrook and its white smock windmill

to the land, serving agriculture or forestry, and you are as likely to meet a tractor as a car. Verges tend to be wide and in spring and summer are bright with flowers. Primroses, violets and mauve cuckoo-flowers colour hedgerow banks in April, red campion mingles with white cow parsley in May, followed by rosebay and greater willow herb, while creamy meadowsweet fills the air with fragrance in damp stretches. Honeysuckle, wild roses and the big white trumpets of convolvulus bloom in hedgerows.

In odd corners by the roadside you will often find half-overgrown ponds. These are no longer of any use to farmers, for modern herds of cattle would never be permitted to take such unhygienic drink as this. Probably the farmers have left the ponds there as a gesture to conservation, perhaps encouraged to do so by the local trust for nature conservation; for these little pools are refuges for wildlife which finds little comfort in today's highly intensive agriculture. They have to be 'managed', however, or they would soon be choked, and often the conservationists undertake to keep them clear. Mallard love the pools, moorhen, coots and sometimes a pair of swans will nest there, foxes, badgers, stoats and weasels drink there, migratory birds are glad to pause for rest in the surrounding shrub and brushwood.

There are also small patches of woodland where the earth is always damp, and in winter wet and soggy. Water wells up in the imprints of your boots, and the air is always cool and moist in the little half-wild and shady areas. The pools and wet woodlands are a reminder that old Andredsweald is not far off. If the hand of man were suddenly withdrawn, the boggy jungle would return in a very short time.

About four miles west of Herstmonceux you come unexpectedly upon Hellingly. With no preliminary distant glimpse to rouse your interest, suddenly you are there and among strong echoes of early Saxon settlers. There they built a circular burial ground, and as they made it, so it has remained. Trees grew, decayed, died, and new trees took their place. Nearby dwellings aged, to be replaced by new and different kinds of dwellings, but always the sacred circle was left untouched. That is how you see it today, still the burial ground, for it is now the churchyard, still the circle whose ancient boundaries you cannot miss. Houses follow the line of the circle but do not intrude into it. Parts of the nearby church date from about 1190. Much is fifteenth century, and a massive tower was added in 1836. One corner bears evidence to a little bit of human frailty. There is a sundial on the south-facing buttress. Somebody some time moved it from somewhere else and replaced it upside down. Upside down it stays today.

A short distance south-east brings you to Horselunges Manor, a magnificent example of fifteenth-century timber framing, surrounded by a moat fed by the Cuckmere River. The strange name is a combination of two names brought together by marriage, de Herst and Lyngyver.

The area immediately north of Hellingly is a remote and seldom-visited land, entirely agricultural, based on livestock and therefore pastoral. The purpose of the lanes which wind through it is to connect farm to farm, with a central point at Cowbeech, grouped round a junction of lanes and as lovely and as agricultural as its name suggests. The '– beech' may be misleading. It may have nothing to do with beech trees. Most of the plentiful trees at Cowbeech are oaks. It could come from the Saxon '*baece*' or '*bece*', a beck or brook, and therefore the stream where cows come to drink. There are no tourist highspots in the neighbourhood, and no shops offering 'souvenirs'. Motorists must be prepared to wait for passing cattle, tractors and riders. In return you find the boon of quietude.

Two miles south of Hellingly, Hailsham all but steps upon the Levels. This is a busy little town with a long history and referred to in Domesday Book as Hamelesham with land for four ploughs. From the church tower belfry, curfew used to be tolled each evening with bells cast nearby. The sound of the bells drifted over the level land and the marshes, bidding farewell to day. Urban development now threatens to join up Hellingly, Hailsham and Polegate, which is already joined to Eastbourne. If so, suburban buildings will hug the eastern end of the Downs all the way from Eastbourne for a total distance of some ten miles.

The picture south-east of Hailsham is altogether more encouraging, for here lie the quiet recesses, rides and tracks of Wilmington Forest, much nearer, in fact, to Hailsham than to Wilmington, which is a downland village. It covers eight hundred acres, and the Forestry Commission bought it in 1953. The nucleus of this forest is very old indeed, a true relic of Andredsweald, and it comprises many different kinds of trees. About a quarter is broadleaved, mostly oak, beech, birch, alder and hornbeam. Various conifers make up the remaining area. Wood ants build their 'pyramids' in open patches and beside the tracks, sometimes up to three feet high. Their building material consists of twigs and forest debris, and the big black insects can be thoroughly belligerent if roused, so don't put your walking-stick into their 'houses'. They do no harm, but on the other hand they do a lot of good by keeping down the caterpillars which could strip the leaves from the oaks.

I recall with great pleasure a sunny afternoon in summer which brought home to me the Commission's responsibility not only to produce timber but also to conserve nature. I came to a clearing where the foresters had deliberately left a luxuriant growth of bramble bushes which bore an abundance of flowers. Hovering and fluttering over the blossom were crowds of gatekeeper butterflies. Their dusky orange contrasted with the white and mauve flowers, which were sometimes almost hidden by the butterflies as they settled on the bushes. Dragonflies shimmered in the sunlight, and a turtle dove purred in a thicket. Rooks, carrion crows, magpies, jays, goldcrests, tits, willow warblers and finches all have their habitats in this very varied forest.

Wilmington Forest belonged to Battle Abbey from the time of Henry I until the dissolution of the monasteries by Henry VIII in 1536. Forestry work was supervised by the abbot, and a part of the forest is still called Abbot's Wood. A track through this wood takes you to a lake which probably supplied fish both to the abbey and to nearby Michelham Priory. There was nobody to care for it after the dissolution, and it was in a sorry state when the Commission took over and, in 1964, gave back to the woods a thoroughly restored lake. Now waterfowl breed upon its banks and herons feed upon its fish.

Walk quietly along the woodland pathways and you may catch a glimpse of badger or fox, particularly at evening or in the early morning. You will notice that replanting has been extensive, necessary to fill the gaps caused by the depredations of two world wars, when huge oaks and beeches were felled in horrifying numbers. Wilmington Forest today is a young forest despite its ancient heart and a few giants here and there, children of the splendid trees once fostered by the abbot of Battle.

Michelham Priory, a little under a mile from the forest, was founded in 1229 by Augustinian canons and was built through the thirteenth and fourteenth centuries. It was practically destroyed after the dissolution and has survived many vicissitudes since. Today it looks more like a mellow manor house than a priory and, in fact, it became a private dwelling after the king's wreckers had finished with it. It passed through many hands before reaching, in 1959, the safe keeping of the Sussex Archaeological Trust. The beautiful, pale sandstone house stands on a seven-acre moat, formed by damming the Cuckmere River. The site was in use before the canons took it over; excavations have revealed what are thought to be part of a Norman manor house. The island may originally have been a Saxon clearing in the forest, *'michel ham'* or *'micel hamm'*, 'large clearing'. *The Oxford Dictionary of English Place Names* suggests that *'micel'* may be a 'rendering into English of a British word for great'. If so it will be one of the rare occasions of Saxons talking over something Celtic.

Two spectacular buildings of the original priory cluster remain. The first is the gatehouse tower, which you cannot miss because you have to pass through it. You couldn't miss it anyway, because it is sixty feet high, and there is no other building in the neighbourhood approaching that height. It was built about 1395, and the stone walls are the originals. The other building is the great barn, whose fourteenth-century structure was extended in the sixteenth century. The magnificent oak and elm timbers inside are mostly the medieval originals. Outside a pretty little terrace overlooks the placid waters of the moat.

The most impressive feature of the countryside from now on is not Wealden but downland. The Downs rise dramatically from the plain, one prominent curve succeeding another, reaching far away to the north-west. They are a presence which you feel as well as see. They are always there as a background. They dominate the landscape, yet they are another land, with an agriculture and a wildlife vastly different from the Weald. The line of demarcation is sharp. A few yards take you into a region of wild thyme, harebells, scabious and rampion which do not grow in the Weald.

The low plain is not flat. It is pleasantly undulating. Meadows and fields lift gently to meet a low sky, and fall back into soft declines. Villages tend to be spacious and often scattered, unlike the villages of the Downs, where deep coombes mould them into compact patterns with houses standing cheek by jowl or in terraces. There are also big greens and commons in the Low Weald, and hamlets are often scattered between the villages.

A group of self-contained and highly individual villages await your discovery immediately you leave Michelham Priory. The first is Arlington, about a mile west of Abbot's Wood, a small scattering of houses, a secluded common, a much visited reservoir and a sturdy flint church whose architecture extends from the Saxon era to the fifteenth century.

A two-mile journey westward brings you to Selmeston. Here, a small group of people looking for somewhere to live found themselves on a sandy ridge sheltered by hazel woods. They liked it, decided to settle and established dwelling places on the ridge. Their remains were found five thousand years later. Professor Graham Clark carried out a scientific investigation in 1933, when he found over 6,400 flint implements in one spot. He also found ashes from fires and even shells from hazelnuts. The dwellings were almost certainly pits roofed over with interwoven hazel rods, and the people who lived there were the mesolithic, middle Stone Age, hunting people. They were succeeded by a group of neolithic colonizers, whose remains were also noted by Professor Clark. Archaeologists consider this one of the most important mesolithic sites to have been discovered so far. You can see it for yourself: a disused sandpit, partly overgrown, beloved of wild birds, down a track beside Selmeston church, which was rebuilt in 1867. Two unusual timber octagonal pillars supporting an arcade closely follow fourteenth-century originals. The church stands on a circular mound which was probably a prehistoric burial ground. Domesday Book records the place as Sielmestone and observed that it had a church, a priest and five serfs. The name derives from Sigelhelm's *tun* (homestead or village).

We leave the shadowy, far-off mesoliths for a community practically contemporary with our own by comparison, the Romans at Ripe. Ripe and its close neighbour, Chalvington, are just over two miles north of Selmeston, and you may well wonder what on earth the Romans were doing in a place like that. There are no traces of town, fortress, villa or even staging post, or, for that matter, of any sizeable road. The neighbourhood seems to have been as quiet then as it is now. The idea of a Roman community of some sort came to me long ago one day in my teens, when I was poring over an Ordnance Survey map of the region, planning a bicycle expedition. I noticed a curious symmetry about the lanes and footpaths, and when I went there I found the symmetry extended through the straight lines of the hedgerows. If you could hover above the place, you would see a pattern of squares and rectangles. This is most uncharacteristic of villages and country districts anywhere in England and certainly in the Weald, with its little, winding ways. I found the answer years later through the work of Mr Ivan D. Margary, the archaeologist. Mr Margary delved deeply into the puzzle of the Ripe squares and rectangles and vividly describes their significance in his book *Roman Ways in the Weald*. He considers they are the shapes and lines of a Roman state land settlement given or rented to retired soldiers and other servants of Rome who wished to end their lives in Britain. There are many such in Italy, but the system at Ripe was the first to be discovered in Britain. It is called 'centuriation' because the land was laid out in units of a hundred *jugera*. A *jugerum* was the area which a man and a team of oxen could plough in a day. Roman pottery has been found in the district.

In the middle of the village there is an enchanting house, full of stout timber and little Tudor bricks set at angles to mark a herringbone pattern. It is called, simply, 'The Old Cottage', which it indubitably is. It was built in 1552.

A little to the north of the Roman land settlement, Chiddingly parish, like ancient Rome itself, occupies seven hills. Their names are Stone Hill, Sun Hill, Thunderer's Hill, Burgh Hill, Holme's Hill, Scraper's Hill and Pick Hill. There is no other resemblance. The area is about as far removed from the conception of Roman planning as it is possible to be. It is the quietest stretch of all this quiet neighbourhood. The focus is, of course, Chiddingly village. You see the spire of the church across the meadows, towering above its screen of trees, 128 feet from the ground, queen of the seven hills. Most of the spires in the district are of wooden shingles. This one is stone, and it catches the subtly changing light as the hours move from dawn to dark. The church, a mixture of old and fairly new, contains a sombre monument to the family of Sir John Jefferay, who was Chief Baron of the Exchequer for Queen Elizabeth I. Sir John built himself a fine mansion, Chiddingly Place. Parts remain in a farmhouse and a magnificent barn which looks distinctly ecclesiastical. It is, in fact, called 'the chapel' but there is no evidence that it has ever been used as such. Sir John died in 1578.

The cottages of the village cluster close together near the church and form a small square. But Chiddingly was not always the sequestered retreat it is today. In the sixteenth century it was a busy centre of the Wealden iron industry, producing guns, bells and firebacks.

A three-mile journey north-west brings you to East Hoathly, a village of charm and interest but cut in half by the London-Eastbourne road, the A22, busy at all times and fiendish at week-ends. You look west from the churchyard towards a stretch of pasture called Terrible Down. The name seems highly inappropriate, for nothing could be more gentle than this tranquil landscape. But upon it King Alfred is said to have inflicted a defeat on the Danes in a battle of such ferocity that the soldiers were up to their knees in blood.

Visitors to the village are always intrigued by the name of a coppice just outside the village: Breeches Wood. A lady of long ago constantly looked askance at the vicar's worn and threadbare breeches. Eventually she could stand it no more. So she gave him a wood, hoping that he would be able to make enough money from timber production to keep himself respectably breeched. The villagers chortled, and never since has anybody ever called that stretch of woodland anything but Breeches Wood.

We now retrace our steps a bit towards the north-western edge of the Roman land settlement and arrive at Laughton, which is not merely one of the more scattered villages in the area but considerably more scattered than most. The motorist hurrying by is scarcely aware of Laughton at all, just one or two houses and a pub. There is a lot more to the village than that but you have to look for it. This was the country of the redoubtable Pelhams, from whom sprang the earls of Chichester. They lived here from 1534 until 1723, when they moved to Stanmer Park on the outskirts of Brighton. First they lived at Laughton Place and then, from about

1600, at Halland Park. What little remains of these stately homes is now, in each case, incorporated in a farmhouse.

Like most of the Laughton buildings, the thirteenth-century church stands alone, though not aloof, down a lane. Under the chancel lies the Pelham family vault in which forty Pelhams lie, including two Prime Ministers. The vault was sealed in 1886. During a restoration in 1883 the church roof of heavy Horsham slabs was replaced by slates. Massive oak beams arrest your attention as you go in. A gigantic yew tree shades the churchyard.

Westward the countryside changes. It becomes less remote and you begin to meet the big village greens and commons. They may be one or the other or a mixture of both. The first of these greens is at Ringer, about four miles from Laughton straight down the pleasant B2124, with the steep green flanks of the Downs on your left. It is a wide and airy space, almost in the centre of the village, ringed about with fine trees, and plenty of room simultaneously for adult organized games and children's spontaneous play, with ample space left to lie on the grass and laze.

It is hard to believe that this well-cared-for countryside was one of the wildest and most squashy regions in the Weald. Daniel Defoe, in his *Tour Through the Whole Island of Great Britain*, comments with horror on the state of the roads: 'I saw an ancient lady, and a lady of very good quality, I assure you, drawn to church in her coach by six oxen; nor was it done in frolick or humour, but from sheer necessity, the way being so stiff and deep that no horses could go in it.' Sir Herbert Springett, who died in 1620, needed eight oxen and a cart to get him to church on time from Broyle Place, two miles away.

Ringmer green has seen turbulent gatherings. Not the least of these was a band of 150 courageous farm workers, who met Lord Gage, High Sheriff for Sussex, in 1830 by appointment on the green to hand him a petition asking that their wages should be raised from 9d. to 2s. 6d. a day, and that the Poor Law overseers should be dismissed for cruelty. They picked out especially the overseer for Ringmer who, they declared, was 'lost to all feelings of humanity'. Lord Gage granted all the requests, and the farm men, according to *The Times*, 'dispersed with hymns and tears of joy'. But they broke up the village grindstone on their way home.

The Reverend Gilbert White, famous for his *The Natural*

History of Selborne, was a frequent visitor to Ringmer in the 1770s. He stayed with his aunt, Mrs Rebecca Snooke, of Delves, on the edge of the green. From this point he could see the long, lovely line of the Downs to perfection, and the view deeply moved him. He made many expeditions to the hills and he wrote, 'Though I have now travelled the Sussex Downs upwards of thirty years, yet I still investigate that chain of majestic mountains with fresh admiration year by year ... you command a noble view of the wild, or weald, on one hand, and the broad downs and sea on the other.'

At Delves, White met Timothy the tortoise, whose personality and habits he studied and wrote about in his famous book. Timothy lived for forty-six years in the Delves garden, and White refused to be parted from him when Mrs Snooke died in 1780, so Timothy went with him to Selborne. You can see his carapace in London's Natural History Museum.

Ringmer church is big and beautiful and architecturally mixed, beginning in the thirteenth century and ending in the twentieth. The tower was built in 1884 and replaced two predecessors which were burnt down. A strangely mutilated tombstone in the churchyard holds your attention. A village butcher of the eighteenth century sharpened his knives on it, and it is therefore called 'the butcher's stone'. There is a wooden memorial to William Martin, whose name should be familiar in every house. He made the first bicycle in England. It had wooden wheels and no chain and is now at Anne of Cleves' House museum in Lewes.

Two Ringmer girls may well have helped shape the history of the United States. In 1672 Gulielma Springett, daughter of Sir William Springett, of Broyle Place, son of Sir Herbert, married William Penn, the Quaker founder of Pennsylvania. Thirty-six years earlier Ann Sadler, daughter of a Ringmer vicar, the Reverend John Sadler, married John Harvard, founder of the American university. The two girls and Timothy take pride of place on the village sign.

Now we turn north-west to the Ouse Valley and the River Ouse, which makes a leisurely progress through watermeadows down to Lewes in a cup of the Downs, and on to Newhaven and the sea. Many brooks and streams feed the river, and I have spent happy hours exploring these slow waterways by canoe. An inquisitive kingfisher often kept me company, cutting swiftly ahead of my bows, pausing on an overhanging branch, to fly on again when I had caught up. Water voles plopped, unfearful, into the water from their bankside habitats. Unseen otters whistled. An owl sometimes watched me pass from a vantage point in a tree, twisting round its neck like a corkscrew. Alders and hazels brush the surface of this stretch of water. Huge white willows tower from the banks of river and brooks and stand in splendid isolation in the middle of the meadows. They are the most conspicuous feature of the landscape, which in many respects resembles Pevensey Levels.

At the centre of this tranquil countryside lies Barcombe. Barcombe is as much a district as a place and you have to walk, drive or cycle quite a bit to make the most of it. You will not regret it. Barcombe village all but died during the time of the Black Death in the fourteenth century. Untenanted cottages fell into disrepair, became overgrown and finally crumbled and collapsed. Presently only mounds in the landscape marked the place where the village had been. The church, a farmhouse, a few of the more substantial cottages and the village pond remained. In due course another village grew up a mile and a half away. This is now called Barcombe Cross, a lively, pretty place, with a good inn, good shops and a beautiful cricket ground. But the map still marks Barcombe where it used to be, and this sometimes leads to bewilderment: people arrive at the church and look around in vain for the village. But it is an idyllic spot. The village pond is still there, but trim lawns now slope to the water's edge from a long red house skilfully converted from unwanted thirteenth-century cottages. The church, much of it eleventh century, contains exquisite woodcarving, and you will always remember the view across the meadows of the Ouse Valley, with the Downs receding gently east and west.

Northward, Uckfield sits on the busy road junction, which, in this age of the fast car, the lorry and the articulated truck, means the banishment of peace and quiet. It is a small town, partly new and partly old; the old is gracious but does not immediately meet the eye.

Until recently it was rare to find a building taken down and reconstructed with absolute exactitude. But it happened at Newick, a few miles west of Uckfield, in 1886-7. The operation was not on a large scale, nor was an entire building involved. But the work was delicate in the highest degree and demanded the utmost skill and care. It was considered desirable to lengthen the nave of the church. So the chancel was taken down and re-assembled about its own length away; and the nave was extended over the intervening space. It cost £3,600, a large sum at that time.

Newick stands about half way between Winchester and Canterbury, and it was a resting place for pilgrims, who stayed at a hostel built in 1510 and run by monks. In due course the hostel became a hotel, called the Bull. This apparently unecclesiastic name is, in fact, an echo of the very ecclesiastic establishment. The sign shows the kind of bull we all know. Once it indicated the papal Bull, which is an edict beginning with the name of the pope; one side of the sign bore the name of the reigning pope, and the other the heads of St Peter and St Paul.

Nearby, Chailey, like Barcombe, is more a district than a place. There are three focal points, South Chailey, Chailey Green and Chailey Common. Chailey Green is the true centre of the original village, now much shrunken in size. The green is small but attractive and is graced by a church begun in the thirteenth century. Its tower bears an unusual spire like a miniature pyramid. Houses and cottages are scattered round the common, a wide and breezy place on the fringe of the Forest Ridge. It is now a nature reserve, having, ironically, been rescued from nature. Its scrub threatened to engulf it when commoners no longer needed it for livestock grazing. Naturalists and local authorities took it over.

On the edge of the common stands the famous Chailey Heritage Craft School and Hospital for physically handicapped children, founded in 1903. Dame Grace Kimmins, one of the principal founders, had the school in her charge for about fifty years. The school and hospital have vastly expanded since her day and are now of national importance in rehabiliating children who are handicapped by physical disability.

A smockmill has crowned the highest point of the common since about the middle of the nineteenth century, a gleaming white landmark for many miles. Its first home was at West Hoathly, high on the Forest Ridge, where its sweeps caught all the winds that blew. It was moved to a downland hilltop, and then to a high point above Newhaven. Then it was taken to Chailey.

Ditchling Common, about four miles away through a series of byways, had to be saved from the commoners, a group of whom wanted to enclose it in order to practise a more intensive agriculture and preserve their cattle from traffic on the fast road which crosses it. But the common had become popular with the public, who had grown to regard it as theirs by right. The strong objection of the public to enclosure was matched by the commoners' determination to enclose. The dispute was eventually settled in 1974, when East Sussex County Council, backed by the Countryside Commission, established 188 acres of the common's 296 as a country park. The remaining 122 acres are fenced in, but the public has rights of access. Ditchling Common is less attractive than Chailey Common, but it has some pleasing features. There is a large pond in the country park section, and spring brings sheets of bluebells and wood anemones, which country people call windflowers.

In the early nineteenth century a much larger common of mingled woodland, heath and rough grass lay immediately to the north. To the west of this open tract lay Cuckfield and to the east Lindfield. Local people called it Hewards Hoth, pronounced 'Yewards Hawth'. The coming of the London-Brighton railway in 1841 changed this countryside completely, and the area is now one of the most populated in the whole Weald. Cuckfield refused a station, so the railway company ran their line two miles east through the 'hawth', and there they built the station, exactly mid-way between Cuckfield and Lindfield. That was the end of the 'hawth'. The station attracted a rush of building, and the open land disappeared under bricks and mortar and spacious gardens, some of them very beautiful. This place is now Haywards Heath, one of the busiest commuter centres on the railway and a thriving town. It developed, however, in bits and pieces and still has no true heart.

Cuckfield and Lindfield have retained their identities, but only just. Haywards Heath constantly threatens to swallow both. Lindfield is the more spacious, with three focal points. At one end of the half-mile street and at its highest point is the church, whose slender, shingled spire soars 116 feet from the ground; at the other end, an ornamental pond which used to be the duck pond, with gardens sloping down to the water's edge; and opposite, across the road, the common, which used to be the goose green and is now the most well tended, lawn-like common you are ever likely to meet.

An architect could profitably spend whole days between church and pond, studying the development of his profession through the ages. There are buildings of many styles, periods and sizes, with much black timber work. Of all the ancient buildings, the most outstanding is Old Place, late sixteenth century, gabled and timber-framed.

You sense all the atmosphere of a small country town at Cuckfield, despite the powerful claims of Haywards Heath upon the shopper. This is no more than just, for Cuckfield's urban traditions reach far back through the centuries. It was granted a charter in 1254. A half-timbered seventeenth-century house at the top end of the High Street was the home of Henry Kingsley, novelist brother of Charles. He is buried in the churchyard, from which there are sweeping views south to the Downs. The church is mostly of the thirteenth and fourteenth centuries.

Unlike Haywards Heath, nearby Burgess Hill was there before the railway came. The station, in the middle of the town, brought great expansion, particularly since the last war, but Burgess Hill was already well established due to its brickworks, nationally known from at least the early eighteenth century and probably before. The town was there even before the brickworks. It became known as Burgess Hill in 1597, taking its name from the Burgey family which is mentioned in taxation records of 1296. Historic houses include Greate Ote Hall, built about 1530. Queen Elizabeth I is said to have stayed there in 1591, and if that does not invest a place with venerable dignity, what does?

The parish church is not only a place for prayer and worship but also a monument to the town's brickmakers. It was built in 1861 entirely of local bricks and tiles, including the spire, and is now scheduled as a building of historical and architectural interest.

The danger now is size. If Burgess Hill and Haywards Heath grow much bigger, they will join up and smother a large chunk of the mid-Sussex Weald. To make matters worse, a sort of secondary conurbation has developed on nearby Hassocks and Hurstpier-point, and if local authorities do not beware there will eventually be a solid mass of buildings from the foot of the Downs to the north of Haywards Heath, over six miles with the railway slicing through the middle or its way to London.

As you make your way westward, you soon find yourself once more in a quiet and retiring countryside, subtly different from the eastern Low Weald but as enchanting. It is more homely and the sense of remoteness is less. It is strongly influenced by the two-pronged River Adur, one prong from the east and the other from the north-west, flowing slowly through flat meadows, attended by many streams and tributaries. The two stretches of water come together slightly west of Henfield, and the river flows serenely on through a gap in the Downs to reach the sea at Shoreham. These pastures are frequently flooded in winter, and naturalists hope that land drainage will not change this, for to these watermeadows come many wildfowl in winter, including Bewick's swans, which have lost their traditional winter refuges elsewhere to agricultural reclamation.

Here, once more, are the winding lanes connecting little-visited villages and hamlets whose interest is frequently far greater than their size suggests.

Albourne is such a village, half hidden by the trees, screened by hedges on tall banks. Scattered about are fine timber-framed houses and cottages. James Starley was born in one of these in 1830. He was a man of great inventive talent. He designed a special kind of two-seater tricycle on which couples sat not one behind the other but side by side. The machine inspired the famous jingle from *Daisy Daisy* of the music halls:

> But you'll look sweet
> upon the seat
> of a bicycle made for two

But before we wander further along the lanes and quiet roads we must visit two small but busy towns, both typical of this part of the Weald but each with its own distinct personality: Henfield and Steyning. Henfield has a large and particularly beautiful common, some of which is left more or less wild, and some, by contrast, given over to an extremely well-maintained cricket ground. Cricket is played here with even more reverence than elsewhere. Henfield without cricket is unthinkable, for the town has had a cricket club since 1771.

The little town is centred on a long, bustling High Street lined with good shops and old, intriguing houses. There are two interesting inns, the George and the White Hart, both eighteenth-century stage-coach hostelries. Superb timber work in the George is the handiwork of fifteenth-century craftsmen. But when you step off the street, either side, you find yourself among narrow pedestrian ways which bound the gardens of handsome houses and pretty cottages, with here and there an unexpected paddock.

There is, however, a grim spot in Henfield's otherwise untroubled history. The plague broke out here in 1609, and sixty people died between 13 September and the following 16 January. A poignant little note in the parish records says, 'Jane Bisshop was borne when the plague was in Henfield and was in her Father's house, and that was the cause that shee was soe long before shee was baptised.'

The Saxons made Henfield a place of some consequence, and the Normans gave it generous space in Domesday. The Saxons called it Hanefeld, which probably meant rocky field; Old English '*hân*' meant rock or stone. About a mile south of the town the Sussex Trust for Nature Conservation has made an ancient millhouse and watermill its headquarters. The Trust has thoroughly restored both house and mill, and from time to time the millwheel spins in its stream and puts into motion the interior mechanism which once ground wheat.

Henfield was always agricultural and still is. But the Saxons of Steyning looked to the sea for their livelihoods. In their day it was an important port. A great estuary lay where now the Adur makes its placid way through pastures down to the coast, and Steyning stood at its head. It was a royal possession and Camden, the sixteenth-century historian, suggested that the town was the Steyningham mentioned in the will of King Alfred. King Alfred's father, Aethelwulf, may be buried at St Andrew's Church, founded by the Saxon St Cuthman in the eighth century. The Normans put their highest architectural genius into the church which they built on the site of St Cuthman's, and this work is now considered some of the best late Norman in the country.

The sea betrayed the Steyning seafarers and merchants in the fourteenth century, just as it betrayed the Romney Marsh ports.

The estuary silted up, and Steyning's fortunes shrank with the tides. The port declined and grew unkempt, like something thrown up by the sea and forgotten. But eventually its people turned their back on the sea and their faces to the land, and Steyning became a thriving agricultural centre.

Steyning High Street is an outstanding example of 'small is beautiful', not the actual street, which is very long, but its composition of small houses and small shops, a medley of black beams, white plaster, red bricks and tiles, and roofs of grey Horsham slabs, with here and there a roof of meticulous thatch. It is a comfortable and homely street, though overfull of traffic, and it is primly presided over by the Market House, a small building with a dainty clock tower.

Still, it is pleasant to get back into the lanes and up to Ashurst, where you find a peculiar kind of trumpet hanging on an inside wall of the church, which sits demurely alone among woods and meadows. It is a vamping horn, a church instrument which came into use in the reign of Charles II. It was a kind of one-man band and was expected to put zip into the congregation's singing, otherwise unaccompanied. The Ashurst horn is made of iron and equipped with a wire framework inside to provide extra resonance. This horn is unique because it is shaped to an angle, a feature lacking in the other half-dozen vamping horns known to exist. But why vamp? The derivation is unexpectedly prosaic. It comes from the French *'avant pied'*, which was a piece of leather on the front of a boot for added strength.

In a little over three miles up the Adur valley you come to West Grinstead. For forty-eight years Hilaire Belloc worshipped in the Roman Catholic church in this scattered village, and he is buried in the churchyard with his wife and son. A simple wooden plaque stands at the head of their graves. The writer and poet died in 1953 when he was eighty.

In a priest's house next to the church you catch an echo of those old, unhappy, far-off days when men persecuted one another in England because of their religious beliefs, Catholic against Protestant, Protestant against Catholic. There, hidden high up in the roof, among the rafters, the Catholics constructed a little chapel where they could celebrate Mass secure from the wrath of seventeenth-century pursuing Protestants. The little refuge was

*Cranbrook church, sometimes called
cathedral of the Weald*

never discovered, and access to it was almost certainly through priests' 'holes', one of which you can see. The chapel is still there.

The Church of England parish church stands alone in a secluded place among meadows and great oaks. The Adur flows close by. The backs of some of the pews still bear the names of farms whose owners habitually sat in them in the early nineteenth century. The church was built in the eleventh century, a small and simple construction, some of which remains.

Two families strongly stamped their influence upon this part of the Weald, the Carylls and the Burrells. The Carylls arrived in 1607, ardent Catholics, and it was largely due to them that the area remained a stronghold of Catholicism when it was highly perilous to have anything to do with it. The Burrells included Sir William, who built up a collection of documents and drawings for a history of Sussex. These are now in the British Museum. Sir William died in 1796.

Nearby Shipley is as unlike West Grinstead as it is possible for two villages to be. The only thing the two have in common is the green, secluded countryside. Shipley is neat and compact and demonstrates how ancient and modern can merge happily. Old houses are grouped together, among old fruit trees in old gardens. New houses are designed to fit comfortably into the traditional pattern.

Two famous men loved Shipley. One was Belloc and the other John Ireland, the composer. Belloc lived in a big, rambling house called King's Land, which he bought in 1906. He had to travel over four miles to the Catholic services at West Grinstead. With the house, Belloc bought a big smockmill, built in 1879, and the meadow in which it stood. The mill is now maintained in his memory by West Sussex County Council. Belloc was born in France, but he found his true home in these tranquil reaches of southern England, and his love of the southern countryside is reflected in his prose and poetry.

John Ireland did not live at Shipley but he was a frequent visitor, increasingly so as the years passed. His great pleasure was to sit in a corner of the churchyard and watch the sunlight play upon a meadow and the River Adur, here little more than a stream, and upon a big and ancient farmhouse at the end of the meadow. He lived at Washington, at the foot of the Downs, and he died in

Bodiam Castle, built in 1385 as a defence
against the French who never attacked it

1962, when he was eighty-three. At his own wish he was buried in Shipley churchyard near the place where he used to sit. A simple uncarved stone stands at the head of his grave, another at the foot.

The Knights Templar built the church in the twelfth century, and some of the Norman interior work indicates very high talent. There are two beautiful arches as you look towards the chancel and there is an exquisite west doorway.

An historic house some five miles west of Shipley sits modestly back in the middle of an orchard, down a long track. It is no grand mansion, no ancestral country seat of some redoubtable knight. It is a long, low-hung and very lovely yeoman's dwelling with walls of black oak and white plaster under a roof of meticulously placed Horsham slabs. Walls had to be strong indeed to support a roof like that.

The house was called Little Slatters, and in the late seventeenth century it was the home of a farmer, John Shaw, a member of the Society of Friends (the Quakers) who suffered great persecution before the Toleration Act of 1668 for insisting on the right to worship freely in their own way. At the invitation of John Shaw, the Friends in the district gathered at Little Slatters one day in May 1682, and that meeting was the forerunner of many similar meetings: of peaceable but determined people gathered together, defying current religious ordinances, refusing to be tongue-tied by authority. Eventually the meetings became regular religious assemblies, and John Shaw converted one end of his house into a specific Friends' meeting house where the Quakers could regularly worship.

One man was particularly outspoken at these meetings, and his eloquent speeches became a powerful influence not only in the local countryside but nationwide. He was William Penn. Penn lived at Warminghurst, four miles from Little Slatters, and he rode over regularly for Sunday worship, often followed by his wife, the Ringmer Gulielma, and their children in an ox-drawn coach. Meetings were also held at Penn's Warminghurst house, with attendances of over two hundred. In this house Penn drafted the Constitution of Pennsylvania with the help of Algernon Sidney, grand-nephew of the famous Sir Philip, of Penshurst Place, in the North Weald, in Kent.

Little Slatters is now called the Blue Idol, and nobody knows how it came by such an improbable name. Perhaps because it was colour-washed in blue between 1793 and 1869, when low attendances had forced its closure, leading possibly to the term 'idle blue meeting-house'. It is now a guest house. The house was built about 1580; extensions have been added with taste and care.

A building very similar to Little Slatters stands immediately outside the churchyard at Thakeham, an easy walk from Warminghurst: Church House, timber-framed with black oak, roof of Horsham slabs, sixteenth-century and very beautiful. The Sandstone church, on a rounded hillock, is large and handsome, and is mostly thirteenth century added to Norman work of which only the nave remains. About 1500 the church was furnished with oak pews ornamented with carved leaves and Tudor roses. Today's congregations use them still. Big fields stretch away to the Downs. It is a peaceful, undiscovered spot.

So is West Chiltington, a short distance north-west. Of the church it has been said that if it were in Italy people would make pilgrimages to it. You see the spire above undulating meadows long before you reach the village. Most of the church was built between fifty and a hundred years after the Conquest, and the spire, added in 1602, is the newest part.

At Storrington you are back in the busy world, but only when in the High Street. Practically all the traffic is going through. It has nothing to do with Storrington. You have but to step off that street either side and you regain the quiet. Leafy byways lead you down to the Anglican parish church built by the Normans and considerably extended later, a Catholic church, a Catholic monastery and the green wall of the Downs. Francis Thompson stayed several years at Storrington, which he dearly loved, and wrote some of his most memorable poetry there, including 'The Hound of Heaven'. In Thompson's day Storrington was a village. Now it is a small town. With a few ugly exceptions, growth has been tasteful and restrained, bit by bit, house by house, through generations, and no blatant blocks challenge the sky.

At Pulborough and Billingshurst you are on Roman ground. When you travel up the dead straight road from one to the other, you follow Roman footsteps, for this is the great highway which connected Noviomagus (Chichester) with Londinium. The Saxons called it Stane (stone) Street, as they did the road driving north from Lympne, and that is what we call it today. Perhaps one day archaeologists will discover what the Romans called these roads. Pulborough and Billingshurst both straddle the highway, now a fast main road. More than once the name, Billingshurst, has been associated with Belinus, possibly a Roman surveyor who may have worked on and perhaps designed the great road. Could the name of the village have been derived from the name of the surveyor? E.V. Lucas notes the suggestion in his *Highways and Byways of Sussex*, written just after the turn of the century. Alas, a more prosaic origin is much more likely: woodland (hurst) belonging to the Saxon tribe Billingas. Traces of Roman life survive in the village. Fragments of Roman brickwork, for instance, went into the building of the church, a big and beautiful place with a magnificent fifteenth-century oak ceiling. Opposite, the Six Bells stands in a garden and reminds you instantly of Church House at Thakeham and the Blue Idol. There is the same type of timber-framed walls with strong perpendiculars and horizontals. It started life in 1320 as a farmhouse.

Echoes of the Roman Empire are strong at Pulborough. Villas have been located in or near the little town and in the immediate neighbourhood. By far the most important of these discoveries has been made at Hardham, a hamlet less than a mile from Pulborough. Here the Romans built a posting station, their first out of Noviomagus and thirteen miles from the city. Here the traveller found accommodation up to high Roman standards, where he could eat, drink and rest in comfort. The station covered just over four acres, and it was probably a Roman-Celtic collection of lodgings, stables, shops and dwellings occupied by the people who ran the station. Mr Margary suggests it was actively in use from about AD 50 to 150. Archaeologists believe it might have been transferred to a higher area where Pulborough church now stands. That would certainly have been more comfortable, for the original site lay where two rivers met, the Arun, flowing from the north, and the Rother from the west, and both given to flooding. They still are. The Rother here is not to be confused with the other, eastern Rother whose countryside we have already explored.

Hardham's humble little church is noted for its murals, painted about 1100, probably the oldest in the country. They take up practically the entire wall space. Their purpose was to convey stories from the Scriptures to people who could neither read nor write, and they made it clear that if you were good enough the blessings of Heaven awaited you, but if you were not the torments of Hell would be your fate.

Half a mile south the ruins of Hardham Priory overlook the Arun watermeadows. It was founded in 1250 for Augustinian canons and was dissolved in 1535 by agreement between the prior and Sir William Goring, the patron. Part of the buildings became a private house. Delicate pillars and bold pointed arches are what remain of an adjoining chapterhouse.

We are now nearing the end of the Low Weald. A mile from Pulborough a medieval stone bridge at Stopham takes the road over the Rother into the Western Weald, but we do not cross it. Wisborough Green, about two miles west of Billingshurst, stands upon the border of the same region. It is an exquisite place, built round a spacious green on the edge of extensive orchards. Trees surround the green, and a tall and slender spire overtops everything. It rises from a church begun about 1100, growing as the years passed. The area supported a glass-making industry from the thirteenth century to the sixteenth. The furnaces, mostly worked by Frenchmen, contributed to the destruction of the Wealden forest.

The countryside ahead beckons invitingly. But we go no further. The narrow clay belt has suddenly ceased to be narrow and low. It has become a wide tract with extensive views, and from it a long arm curls north-east round Horsham and the Forest Ridge.

To the Forest Ridge we now turn.

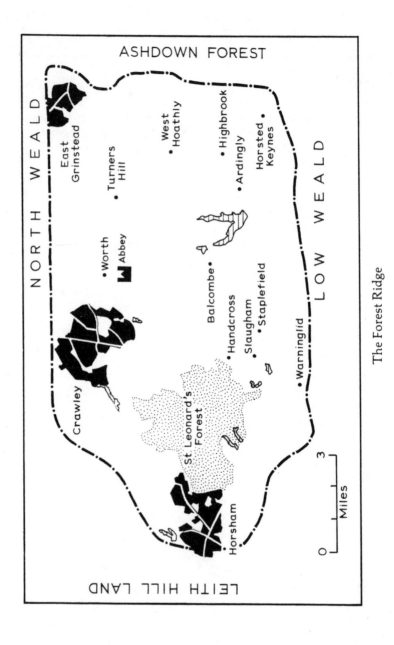

The Forest Ridge

8

The Forest Ridge

This region is well named. It is lavishly forested. Trees are the outstanding feature. You feel that villages and even the three towns, Horsham, Crawley and East Grinstead, are there by permission of the trees. Small farms appear as clearings, which, indeed, most of them once were; you get the impression that the meadows and small fields properly belong to the trees, and that the trees might one day advance and reclaim the land if they felt inclined. As you make your way along the lanes, roads and footpaths, you often seem to be travelling in a green light through cascades of leaves.

The term 'ridge' is not altogether accurate. There is not just one ridge but a number of ridges, with attendant valleys running parallel with one another. Country people have a habit of simplifying such a complex by lumping it under a singular noun. A similar example is the entire range of the South Downs, which the countryman calls the hill.

There are ten miles of this high, wooded area reaching from Horsham and St Leonard's Forest to East Grinstead and the western end of Ashdown Forest. You cannot pick it out on the geological map, but it comprises the western end of the area which is surrounded by the Wealden clay, and you will see from the map that this is almost entirely Tunbridge Wells sand with a few smatterings of Wadhurst clay. Sand here is, of course, a geological term. The soil of the Forest Ridge is what most of us would call loam, and it is highly fertile. Yet, apart from the splendour of the trees, the main characteristic of the region is great outcrops of sandstone rock. You come upon them unexpectedly in the woods. They shore up valleys and occasionally they stand apart, in splendid isolation. They gleam orange in the sun and glisten black in the rain.

Both oaks and beeches thrive in the loam soil; both achieve

majestic proportions and they comprise the majority of the trees in
this heavily wooded upland. They stand not only in impressive
assemblies but also singly, beside roads and lanes, along field
hedgerows and frequently in meadows. They are beautiful at all
times of the year, strong silhouettes in winter, dark green canopies
in summer, bronze and russet in autumn relieved by the vivid
yellow of birches, but loveliest of all in spring, when the young
beech leaves are a bright, transparent green and shimmer in the
sun, and the oaks are mingled green and gold. In early summer
rhododendrons suddenly erupt in a blaze of reds, mauves and
vivid whites. Through the boughs of the trees in any season you
can watch the sunlight play and shift on the fields of the Low
Weald below and upon the flanks of the Downs rising sharply
from the lower land.

Horsham is very much a town of the woodlands. All the
approaches are wooded, and even when you are in the heart of the
town, heavily timbered walls remind you of the forests just beyond
the town boundaries. The name itself has a true Saxon country
ring, Hors-ham, an enclosure for horses. That is how it was once
pronounced, and not, as it is universally mis-pronounced today,
Hor-sham. The central area, called the Carfax, remains much as it
always has been since Horsham became a town. The unusual name
probably derives from the Latin *quadrifurcus*, four streets, though
today not four but six streets radiate from this focal point. Oxford
is the only other town in England with a Carfax. The streets are
unspectacular, busy and pleasant, and, despite the surge of traffic
through it, the town still maintains much of the grace and unhaste
of the country town of long ago. There is change, of course.
Modern buildings have appeared, but they have been sited
carefully, and the clash between old and new is less here than in
many, perhaps most, places.

One area remains almost completely untouched. This is the
Causeway, a broad cul-de-sac with the turreted and grim-faced
town hall at one end and the partly Norman, partly Early English
church at the other. Entry from the Carfax is inconspicuous and
easily overlooked. You have the choice of an alley either side of the
town hall, and you pass immediately from an age of bustle into an
age of quiet and dignity. Lime trees line a pleasant boulevard, there
is no other name for it, and the houses are so lovely that it seems

Pevensey Levels: protected by the
Nature Conservancy Council

Frieze of reeds: an evening prospect on Pevensey Levels

invidious to pick out only one for comment. Causeway House, however, is outstanding, though not to such an extent that its companions seem diminished by comparison. It was built about the middle of the sixteenth century, dark timber, white plaster and gables. It houses the Horsham Museum, which is more a demonstration of rural social history than a conventional museum.

A plain memorial slab in the church commemorates the poet Shelley, who was born at nearby Field Place in 1792 and was drowned off the coast of Italy on 8 July 1822, while sailing near La Spezia. Ironically, he was then working on his poem 'The Triumph of Life', which was published after his death, incomplete.

By far the most prominent feature of the church is its spire, which soars 230 feet from the ground, a marvellous picture on a bright day with a blue and white sky behind it, its fifty thousand wooden shingles gleaming in the sun. The paths of the churchyard, laid with Horsham slabs, lead you to a secluded Garden of Remembrance, flanked by the Arun, with playing fields the other side, and then the open country. This is one of the great charms of Horsham, how suddenly you are off the streets and into woods and fields.

Horsham may well have been firmly established as a settlement before the Normans arrived, but it is not mentioned in Domesday; and though it had achieved the status of borough by 1236, it was never granted a charter of incorporation. Nevertheless, Horsham was represented by two Members of Parliament from 1295 until the Reform Act of 1832. Assizes were held in the town from 1306 until 1830, but by that time the town had declined in both status and commercial importance and was described in 1830 as having the appearance more of a village than a town. Now the pendulum has swung again. Horsham has become popular as a place to live in, and as a place from which to commute to London; it has a vigorous business and social life of its own; national enterprises have chosen Horsham as their headquarters rather than any of the big cities. It would be a pity, however, if it were to fall a victim to the current craze to expand. If it did, the very qualities which now make the town so pleasant would be lost under the pressure of bricks and concrete.

At the town's eastern end about a mile from the Carfax, the leaves of St Leonard's Forest all but brush the roofs of the houses.

The smockmill at Shipley which
Hilaire Belloc bought

Into the glades, recesses and little pathways of this forest we now venture.

At one time this would have been considered a reckless thing to do. In the summer of 1614 a number of people claimed to have seen, independently, a terrifying reptile. Three of these observers wrote down in detail their experiences, signing their story, 'John Steele, Christopher Holden and Widow Woman dwelling near Faygate'. They said of the monster that there 'is always in his tracks or path left a glutinous and slimie matter ... which is very corrupt and offensive to the scent'. Its length was estimated to be 'nine feete, or rather more. The scales along his backe seem to be blackish, and so much as is discovered under his bellie, appeareth to be red ... It is likewise discovered to have large feete, but the eye may be there deceived ... He is of countenance very proud, and at the sight or hearing of men or cattel, will raise his neck upright and seem to listen and looke about with great arrogancy.' The monster spat venom, 'as was proved on the bodies of a man and a woman ... found dead, being poysoned and very much swelled, but not prayed upon'. Two mastiff dogs were killed, but 'were not prayed upon, but slaine and left whole; for his food is thought to be, for the most part in a conie-warren', which was found 'much scanted and impaired'. (A conie, or cony, is a rabbit, and the term is still used by country people.)

The objectiveness of the report suggests strongly that John Steele, Christopher Holden and the Widow Woman were not victims of a delusion. They were anxious to stick to facts. They could not be sure whether the creature had feet, and they said so. They also admit to uncertainty about colour.

E.V. Lucas is forthright in his *Highways and Byways of Sussex*: 'Such a story must have had a basis of some kind. A printed narrative such as this would hardly have proceeded from a clear sky.' Sheila Kaye-Smith proffers a definite opinion in *Weald of Kent and Sussex*. A large snake, she guesses, not an English snake, but a snake which may have been brought from abroad by a collector when small, and escaped when full grown. The record is printed in the *Harleian Miscellany*, a reprint of a selection of tracts from the library of Edward Harley, second Earl of Oxford, published in 1744.

St Leonard's Forest is Forestry Commission land, and it is the policy of the Commission to keep its woodlands open to the public provided they do no damage and keep out of young plantations. In St Leonard's Forest there are both old and young trees, both commercial timber and trees left to grow as they please. There are venerable pines, oaks, beeches and birches from which planks will never be made, but how beautiful they are, their boughs bending low over the rough grasses and the brambles that grow around their trunks; and there are stands in which the trees have been induced through skilled forestry to grow tall and straight to meet the timber merchants' needs. In little clearings clumps of heather and rosebay grow, and in thickets in spring nightingales sing both by night and by day, and woe betide any forester who, unknowingly, cuts back the thickets too close for the nightingale's convenience. The infamy of such conduct is immediately pointed out by human residents of the neighbourhood, and the work is stopped or postponed, an excellent example of cultivation hand in hand with conservation.

The iron industry claimed the whole of the Forest Ridge, and St Leonard's Forest, one of the more dense areas in the old Weald, was eventually all but clear felled, the landscape was reduced to a shocking state, and roads became practically impassable due to the teams of oxen dragging timber to the furnaces. John Leland, the sixteenth-century historian, complains that the roads both in and around Horsham were 'full of dyrt and myre'.

Two very large hammer ponds which cut deep into the forest on its southern side, both about half a mile long, are reminders of the Wealden industrial era. Today, surrounded by trees and shrubs, they are peaceful and quiet. Apart from a passing jet up from Gatwick, the only sounds are cries of moorhen and duck.

Not only has St Leonard's Forest had a serpent. It also has a ghost, William Powlett, a captain of the Horse Grenadiers in the reign of George I. Captain Powlett lies in a tomb in West Grinstead church but will not rest there. He rides in St Leonard's Forest, emerging at dusk, headless, not on his own horse but ready to mount any other horse passing by, seating himself on the crupper and flinging his arms round the rider's waist. Poor Powlett must have had a lonely time through the years when the car lorded it in both business and recreation. But the horse is back in favour for recreation. Will Powlett ride again?

Forests continue eastward from St Leonard's, running into one another, Tilgate, Brantridge, Balcombe and Worth Forests, all privately owned but intersected by paths. The main London-Brighton road slashes through, but it is forgotten a short distance either side. To the north the woodlands skirt Crawley, one of the first of the post-war specifically planned new towns. It has not swallowed the original old town. On the contrary, old town and new have somehow come together amicably. Each has its own personality, yet the two have fused into one entity. The old High Street remains the focal point, and here you find architectural styles from the fifteenth century onwards, with much sturdy timber work. The grass-surrounded new buildings are tall but not tall enough to dwarf into insignificance the immediate surroundings. There are also long, low rows of shops – but not long enough or low enough to be boring, though here and there you may sense a certain sameness, but to counter that you also find a blessed sense of space and a freedom from constriction. However, there is a price. If Crawley is allowed uncontrolled expansion, it will reach Horley, and Horley, going in the same direction, north, will merge with Redhill and Reigate, and there will then be an unbroken built-up area from London to the middle of the Weald. From this nightmare I recoil. Let us return to the trees and the villages hidden among them.

These villages are mostly small to medium in size, and practically all are on unclassified lanes or B-roads. They are also distinguished by the greatest concentration you are ever likely to find of roofs of Horsham slabs. We have already noted such roofs in other areas, but here they are at their most numerous and also at their best. There is good reason for this. The Horsham area is the source of the stone. This is where it was quarried. There were quarries in other parts of the Weald, but they were richest around Horsham, which is how the stone came by its name. It is a calcareous sandstone, often rippled, and a single slab may weigh half a hundredweight. Its silver-grey colour is often set off by little clumps of amber moss which gather as the stone weathers. Horsham slabs have also been used for flooring. They may also be called tiles or slate, or simply Horsham stone.

The villages are numerous, but when you are in any one of them there might be no other in the entire Weald, so self-contained and secluded are they in their woodland world. Even Handcross, which you might suppose to be veritable bedlam, since it stands on the London-Brighton highway, is reasonably quiet, for the road is taken through a deep cutting. The village, once choked with traffic at week-ends, now stands high above the streaming lines of metal.

Nearby Slaugham, pronounced 'Slaffham', could be called a showplace except that the villagers have made it so simply for the love of it. Venerable houses with well-kept gardens surround an undulating green, and in the church beside it you will find a Norman font made of that same kind of marble which we have already seen at Bethersden, in the Kentish part of the Weald. Here it is called Sussex marble. In a valley a short distance to the south-east stand the ruins of Jacobean Slaugham Place, family home of the Coverts in the sixteenth and seventeenth centuries, whose estates were said to have extended from Southwark to the sea, but that was no doubt something of an exaggeration. Staplefield, also arranged round a green, is now another quiet retreat but once its life revolved round a busy tannery, and the memory of it is perpetuated in the name Tanyard Lane. It is a big green, cricket is played on it, and it was surrounded by cherry trees when the stage-coaches ran from London to Brighton. Passengers picked the black fruit. Tennyson lived at nearby Warninglid for a short time after his marriage in 1850. The four villages form a sort of natural quartet, though each has its definite identity.

The first building we see as we approach the village of Balcombe, east of Staplefield, is the church, perched high on a bank alone and well apart from the village, rebuilt in 1847-72 except for the tower, which is fifteenth century. Commuters on the Brighton–London railway line are familiar with the 'little church' across the meadows. When you see it at close quarters, you find it a sizeable place. About two miles before they reach this railway viewpoint, commuters have crossed the viaduct which spans the Ouse Valley. This has become something of a tourist attraction, and you can see it best from the narrow, unclassified road to Haywards Heath. It is, 1,475 feet long and the highest point is 119 feet from the foundations and 96 feet from ground level. Eleven million bricks and forty thousand cubic feet of masonry were used in its construction. The bricks are Dutch, and they were brought by sea to Newhaven and then up the Ouse by barge direct to the site, where today the river is not much more than a big ditch. The viaduct was opened to trains on 12 July, 1841.

The centre of Balcombe is a neat square. A lane emerges from it and suddenly dives precipitously, about five in one, in places probably steeper, and you go down and down and eventually come to a millhouse and a sheet of water in a deep valley, the Ardingly reservoir, 180 acres of clear water imaginatively designed in two long prongs and built between 1974 and 1977. It has become a favourite spot for an outing during a sunny week-end.

The lane winds up the other side of the valley as steeply as it came down from Balcombe, often enclosed by large sandstone outcrops. You pass Ardingly church, a massive building, most of it early to middle fourteenth century, and when you reach the village, you turn left. In less than two miles you are at Wakehurst Place, built about 1590 and altered in the years 1845-69. This mansion entirely lacks the sombre character of so many of its stately fellows. It is pleasant to look at, a friendly place, with an air of lightness and grace. But the greatest glory of Wakehurst is the 540-acre estate surrounding the house. Both mansion and grounds are the property of the National Trust, which leases them at a nominal rent to the Ministry of Agriculture for the use of the Royal Botanic Gardens, Kew. Wakehurst is both an annexe to Kew and an important horticultural centre in its own right. It is also highly popular with visitors. It is full of colour from early spring until late autumn. Sheets of daffodils and bluebells give way to foxgloves and flowering shrubs, and in the autumn comes the splendour of the leaves. A previous owner, Sir Gerald Loder, later Lord Wakehurst, made Wakehurst horticulturally famous with a magnificent collection of trees and shrubs assembled from all parts of the world. He was more than a collector, however. He was highly talented and he knew how to display his specimens not only to their own best advantage but also so that they should harmonize with the native trees of the Forest Ridge. This balance is carefully maintained today. The great delight of Wakehurst is its naturalness, which, in fact, owes much to human skill. Nature is guided but never bulldozed. Exotic trees, shrubs and other plants grow happily among the Wealden beeches, oaks, birches and pines. Lakes and dramatic outcrops of sandstone set off the trees and flowers.

We shall now make our way further eastward to Horsted Keynes, which many think is the most lovely of all the Forest Ridge villages. There is certainly none more secluded. A maze of uphill lanes converges upon it, and you arrive with a sense of delighted surprise. You had not supposed a village could be anywhere near. It just breaks upon you, and you love it at once. The first thing you see is a wide and airy green surrounded by cottages, shops, two inns and a former farmhouse, now a private home, and opposite there is a former forge. Half-hidden streams cut through the broken countryside around. Lakes lie among woods and at the base of steep pastures. You feel a space had to be cleared for the village, which understandably is what did happen a very long time ago.

You go down a hill from the green to a Norman church and the oldest cottages, a delectable corner graced by the church's slender, shingled spire. In a recess in the chancel lies a tiny thirteenth-century effigy of a crusader knight, not much more than two feet long including the lion at his feet. The most ancient building in the village apart from the church is a thirteenth-century former priest house, now two cottages, at one end of the churchyard. You can drive no further. The lane becomes a track. Beyond are woods and lakes.

From this Wealden recess there emerged in the seventeenth century a social record now known and valued by social historians throughout the land. The Reverend Giles Moore, rector from 1656 to 1680, kept a daybook, and of this, in 1939, another rector, the Reverend Frank Eardley, wrote in his book *Horsted Keynes* that Giles Moore threw 'quite incidentally, valuable light on the administration of the land, the state of the Church, the social conditions of the people, the postal arrangements of the country, the prices of commodities, and many other characteristics of seventeenth-century England'.

Not only is Giles Moore revealed as a man of careful business habits. He is also seen as somewhat sceptical concerning his parishioners. For instance, 'Never compound with any parishioner till you have first viewed their land, and seen what corne they have upon it that year and may have upon it ye next.'

The name of the village is a mingling of Saxon and Norman. First it was simply Horstede, a place where horses were kept. Then a knight of William the Conqueror, William de Cahaignes, took it over and it became Horstede de Cahaignes.

From some points on the outskirts of Horsted Keynes you can see, on the north-west horizon, a tall spire reaching high above the trees. This is the spire of West Hoathly church, and to West Hoathly we shall now make our way.

The lane we follow winds up the highest part of the Forest Ridge. It is lined by banks, hedges and magnificent free-standing trees, with occasional gaps, through which you catch glimpses of deep coombes and wide prospects of startling beauty. The lane does a loop, and suddenly you find yourself in the centre of West Hoathly, with the church and the Cat Inn one side and the manor house, priest house and old parsonage opposite, all snug and compact and with no sense of altitude. But when you walk through the churchyard, the ground practically drops away from under your feet and the unimpeded view before you takes in woodlands, valleys, churches and farmstead to the long line of the Downs on the southern horizon.

The church has grown from a small building erected twenty-four years after William and his Normans arrived, and some of this early church remains. Holes in the main door and small scars on the turret are said to have been caused by bullets during skirmishes between Roundheads and Cavaliers in the Civil War. A great chest carved out of a single log in the twelfth century is placed just inside the door. The works of the church clock are among the oldest in the country, about 1410-22. The outside dial was fixed early in the nineteenth century, and it upset E.V. Lucas, who complained it was 'the kind of dial that one expects to see outside a railway station'.

The priest house is now a museum in the care of the Sussex Archaeological Trust, who took it over in 1935. It is a fine example of massive timber-framed walls supporting a roof of meticulously placed Horsham slabs, with spectacular beams inside. It was probably built towards the end of the fourteenth century for the great Cluniac priory at Lewes, but for most of its life it was the home of yeomen, and the Trust maintains it as a farmhouse or better-class cottage during the eighteenth and nineteenth centuries, up to about 1850. It does this with great success and exemplary taste. A farmer's wife living in those times would feel perfectly at home walking in today, and might well linger in the parlour with a smile of appreciation for the vases of flowers from the garden outside, where the flowers grow up to window height.

Gravetye Manor, about a mile north if you walk by footpath, rather longer if you drive, is famed for the gardens created by William Robinson, who started his working life at Kew as a garden boy and eventually bought Gravetye in 1885. He put his talents to work not only in the gardens but also in the surrounding woodlands, encouraging native trees and introducing with discretion exotic specimens from overseas. The present big stone manor house was built by a prosperous ironfounder, Richard Infield, in 1597. It took the place of a smaller half-timbered house. Robinson left his estate in trust in 1935, and since then it has been in the care of the Forestry Commission. The woodlands are open to the public. The house is now a hotel, and it overlooks a lake which was once a hammer pond.

In little more than a mile east as the crow flies another sheet of water lies in another deep valley, but as we are not crows we have to follow $2\frac{1}{2}$ miles of lanes, nothing to complain about in this idyllic countryside. Meadows slope down to the water where aquatic plants grow abundantly. Big willows grace the banks. But this lake is not a former hammer pond. It is a reservoir, opened in the early 'fifties and named the Weirwood Reservoir. It is also a nature reserve, partly by official designation and partly because wild creatures have decided they like it and have made their homes there. Uninvited, though certainly welcome, great crested grebes appeared and now breed there, and Weirwood has become one of the best places in the south-east to see these interesting birds. Canada geese also breed there. Herons fish the shallow water by the banks. Large numbers of wildfowl from the north find refuge there in winter.

There are big sandstone outcrops on the higher ground, relics of the sand bed of that other, ancient Wealden lake. From the distance you see a line of tall rocks which look like Easter Island statues. At close quarters you see a jumble of rocks of many shapes, some big, some small. Some seem to have had expressions frozen upon them in far antiquity. They seem to have nothing to do with the lush green landscape.

A lane winds away from the valley and the rocks and goes on

being a lane until it drops you in East Grinstead High Street. Every so often you have glimpses of high, rough ground, the western spurs of Ashdown Forest and a reminder that you are now at the eastern end of the Forest Ridge.

Though East Grinstead is a medley of ancient and modern, it is the ancient which is the more prominent, at least in the High Street, which is long, wide and handsome, and also noisy, on account of traffic. There are dark timbers, both perpendicular and horizontal, in the walls of many Tudor buildings. Much of the timber in doorways and at corners has been worn smooth by the touch of innumerable hands through the centuries. Tall chimneys rise above roofs of Horsham slabs. Upper storeys overhang pavements. Little houses and larger buildings sit side by side without discord.

The most outstanding building is the parish church, whose pinnacled tower rises high above all other buildings and can be seen from far distances, including many points on Ashdown Forest. A previous tower was destroyed in 1683, when lightning struck the steeple and set fire to the wooden shingles. It was soon replaced, but the new tower collapsed in 1785, doing so much damage that the whole church had to be rebuilt. This took from 1789 to 1813, and the work included yet another new tower. The material chosen was local sandstone, pale gold and grey, and it is a handsome and dignified piece of work just off the High Street.

At the eastern end of the High Street, just before you join the Lewes road, the warm sandstone buildings of Sackville College surround a spacious quadrangle. The college was founded in 1609 and completed in 1619 by Robert, second Earl of Dorset and head of the Sackville family, not as an educational institution but as a haven for the old, poor and disabled, for the term 'college' was used far more then for such a purpose than it is today.

But the best-known building in East Grinstead is the Queen Victoria Hospital, built in 1936, famed the world over for its brilliant plastic surgery during the last war and since.

It is an easy matter to get to London by train from East Grinstead, and large numbers of business people do so every day. Once you could also go by train from East Grinstead to Lewes. It was a sort of leisurely, fairy-tale line, a single track nearly all the way, through woods and undulating pasture. Farm houses, herds of cattle, horses and tractors, slid slowly by your carriage window. Crows perched on posts only yards away. Wild flowers grew thickly on the banks and crept down to the very edge of the track.

The little railway was axed in 1955. It was not 'economic'. A small stretch survived between Horsted Keynes and Sheffield Park through the enterprise of a small private company who called their acquisition the Bluebell Railway. This is now a popular tourist attraction.

I still treasure the memory of those unhasty journeys through the quiet countryside, to be precipitated, if you came up from Lewes, with a kind of pleasurable shock into the bustling little market town of East Grinstead. Then, as now, beyond the rooftops you caught glimpses of the high shoulders of Ashdown Forest, and we will now respond to those tantalizing glimpses and set out to explore a region quite unlike any we have so far seen. We soon realize that, despite its name, Ashdown Forest is less forest than moor and heathland.

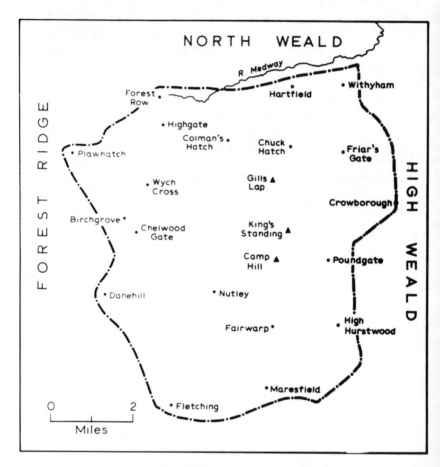

Ashdown Forest

9

Ashdown Forest

It is due to the stubborn determination of the Ashdown Forest commoners that any part of the forest is left open for us to enjoy. Had they been less tenacious and more submissive, the whole lot would have been enclosed centuries ago. As it is, Ashdown Forest is now one of the finest tracts of open heathland in south-east England, mingled with extensive woodlands, both hardwoods and conifers, a place of winds, wildlife and vast views. It marks the exact centre of the Weald.

Thanks to the conservation-mindedness of the Forestry Commission, Ashdown Forest is, in effect, expanding, for large tracts of the Commission's land lie more or less alongside Ashdown, and large areas of this land is open to the public. You walk from one to the other, and no matter what the ownership, you see the countryside as a natural entity, passing from high moorland to lower slopes clad with true forest. It is, however, the breezy upland heathlands on the plateau that are the most distinguishing features of Ashdown Forest; nobody speaks of walking in the Forest, but on the Forest. Because of its altitude, Ashdown Forest was probably less of a jungly tangle than the lower lands of Andredsweald. The neolithic peoples hunted the area but no traces have been found of their having lived there. The Iron Age Celts, however, left various traces of habitations here and there. They were probably temporary camping sites with earthen walls to keep wild animals out, and used to shelter adventurers who penetrated into the wilderness in search of iron. They would have come from the comparatively comfortable villages on the downland hilltops some fourteen miles away, and probably they often yearned to be back among those more open spaces, where danger could be detected in time to take defensive action.

The Romans drove their London-Lewes road by King's Standing and Gills Lap about AD 100, and transport of iron from this region to London or the coast became a moderately straightforward matter. Long stretches of the road can still be walked over. The Sussex Archaeological Trust owns a very well preserved section of it at Holtye, near Hartfield. Roman tracks also cross some of the more westward areas of the Forest, and at least one on the eastern side in addition to the road. They follow ridgeways and were almost certainly there long before the arrival of the Romans, who improved them. These tracks connected with the London-Lewes road, where depots would have been established to receive the iron.

The Romans went. The Saxons came and in their rough way began to open up this slightly less hostile part of the wilderness. They gave it a name, *'aescen dun'*, which would normally have meant 'ash trees hill'. But the ash is uncommon on Ashdown Forest. The name could mean Aesc's hill. Who or what was Aesc? They probably developed a system of common rights in the area, which became firmly based in a peasant economy. When the Normans took over England, they wisely left *aescen dun* alone. To do otherwise would have caused disruption, hardship, probably starvation and done nobody any good, least of all the Normans, who would have added to the reservoir of hatred against them. The place is not even mentioned in Domesday Book. So the commoners continued to enjoy their rights, and changes of remote ownership meant little to them. These common rights included grazing for livestock and a certain amount of timber for fuel.

The kings of England hunted the area following the Norman conquest, but by no means all the deer ended up as venison on their tables or the tables of their friends. They might have claimed it as their own, but the men of the countryside, whose Saxon forefathers wrested a living from the woodlands and the open heaths, had other ideas. They scorned the term 'poacher' and the prevailing drastic penalties for poaching, but they hunted with caution, and they hunted for food and not fun.

In 1372 King Edward III gave the Forest, then as now about fourteen thousand acres, to his third son, John of Gaunt, Duke of Lancaster, who seems to have developed an affection for it and carefully conserved it as a hunting chase. It became known as Lancaster Great Park, and it was officially designated a royal chase. The Duke enlarged a royal hunting lodge which stood somewhere near Nutley. Nobody knows exactly where, but several sites have been suggested.

There is a strong local tradition that the Duke gave refuge and protection to John Wycliffe from those in authority who could not stomach the famous preacher's controversial reforming views. Wycliffe is said to have preached in the district, but again, nobody knows where he stayed or where he preached. It does seem clear, however, that there was a chapel in a wood about half a mile west of Nutley. The wood is still called Chapel Wood, and in account books at Maresfield church there is a reference to 'a chalyce sometyme belonging to the Chepelle of Notley'.

John of Gaunt died in 1399, but life for the forest commoners went on much as before. From time to time they were pushed around as the generations passed, but by and large their rights were respected and it was not until Charles II came to the throne in 1660 that anything happened seriously to disturb them. Rather as gifts from a grateful king, 'improvers' arrived to split up the land, disafforest it and systematically enclose it. The commoners saw themselves entirely banished from their woodlands and grazing, as they certainly would have been. They rose as one man. They tore down the fences. They trampled to death the newly planted hedges. They filled in the newly dug ditches. The improvers complained of 'the crossness of the neighbourhood'. It was a long and bitter fight but in the end the commoners won. In 1693 a Royal Commission awarded 6,400 acres for the use and enjoyment of the commoners, and that is about the extent of the open land to this day. A map was published showing who had rights over what and how much, and a copy of this map is kept at the headquarters of the Ashdown Forest Conservators on the Forest about a mile from Wych Cross. From it you can still clearly recognize the boundaries of the Forest we know today, including certain places at which it was entered through the pale fence which surrounded it, such as Chelwood Gate, Highgate, Poundgate, Coleman's Hatch, Chuck Hatch, Plawhatch.

The award brought to the commoners the legal right to graze their stock, cut a certain amount of light wood for their personal use and cut bracken and heather for livestock bedding. The actual soil of the Forest was the property of the lord of the manor. Friction continued periodically, now between commoners and lord, culminating in a great law action in 1881 which the commoners again won. The result was an Act of Parliament, passed in 1885, clearly setting out the rights and duties of both sides. A board of Conservators was set up to administer the Forest, and this system continues today. Another Act passed in 1974 required the Conservators not only to protect the rights of the commoners but also to maintain the forest 'as a quiet and natural area of outstanding beauty' to which the public is admitted for recreation and enjoyment. The commoners, in standing up for their own rights, also won a magnificent countryside boon for posterity.

It would be a mistake to suppose that Ashdown Forest is now divided into two clear-cut blocks, the public and the private. The two are inextricably mingled, a big stretch of heathland here, an enclosure there. Farms and smallholdings are dotted about the heather but are nevertheless curiously hidden. They do not mar the wild landscape. They do not even look incongruous. They belong. They are part of the Forest, and their cottages and buildings have almost always been built of the golden sandstone to be picked up within a stone's throw, and seem to have sprung unaided from the virgin soil.

Despite all the litigation and legislation, the influence of man has not pressed heavily upon Ashdown Forest. The open area has never felt the bite of the plough, which it certainly would have if the improvers had taken over from the commoners. No drainage schemes have ever sucked the moisture from the valleys. No forestry schemes have ever invaded the high moorland. No matter how often you go there, it always seems new, and always a place apart. The Forest does not claim you, and you do not claim the Forest. You are always a visitor. But it fascinates. It is irresistible. It puts on a different face for morning, mid-day and evening, and also for the changing seasons of the year. I like it best in early morning in spring or summer, when new grass shoots thrust through last year's brown tor grass, bright green tips appear on the heather, the young bracken is unfolding like so many miniature snakes, and vegetation is covered with dew, each globule reflecting the sun. This is the time when you are most likely to meet the wild creatures of the Forest, a fallow deer perhaps, more likely a fox. On such a morning I stood still and watched the biggest fox I have ever seen in my life. What breeze there was blew from the fox to

Cottages at Hellingly follow the circular boundary round a Saxon burial ground, now the churchyard

Low Weald landscape. The photograph was taken near Wivelsfield

me, and as foxes have poor sight, the animal, a lightish russet, was completely unaware of me. It strolled about, unhurried, sniffing this and that, savouring the stillness of the morning, and then strolled casually away.

In summer dark greens replace the bright colours of spring, but towards the summer's end a new brilliance appears. The heather bursts into purple glory. That is followed by a pageant of colour, when woods, coppices and free-standing trees throw off their dark greens for the mingled yellows, reds and bronzes of autumn. The Forest is a sombre and brooding place in winter, but frost and snow can bring about a spectacular transformation. The high moorland becomes a tundra. It is a magnificent sight. Under an icy blue sky and a cold yellow sun it glitters with innumerable points of vivid light. Frost sparkles on needles of pine and reflects into your eyes from heather and seared bracken. The flashing white of the frost and the snow invests even the silver birches with an added brightness. Little slivers of wind cut your face but fill your lungs with vigour.

But Ashdown Forest is wildest in the south-west gales which periodically sweep across it. Then the wild moor is almost forbidding. I once stood on the south-eastern edge of the plateau where it begins to slope down to the Low Weald, and watched the clouds build up the other side. The evening quickly darkened, and soon the whole sky was rushing by, trailing long grey tatters that sometimes swept through the treetops. Trees, bushes, heather and grass bent before the wind, which seemed almost physical in its force and filled the air with noise; and in the tumult I heard a curlew cry.

The highest points of the Forest are at its eastern end, and the actual highest is King's Standing, 715 feet, if you exclude Beacon Hill in Crowborough, 792 feet, as I think you must, since it is now more Crowborough than Ashdown Forest. King's Standing is marked by a stand of Scots pines first planted within an existing square enclosure in 1816. The banks of the enclosure are thought to be the remains, or perhaps the successors, of an enclosure within which some structure stood. It might have been a shelter from which kings watched the deer driven past them, and there is a local tradition that King Edward II did use this point as an observation post. On a map of 1813 it is marked as 'King James's

Woodland at Wakehurst Palace, Ardingly

Standing'. On the 1693 map it is shown as 'Kinges Stand'.

The clump of King's Standing pines is not particularly prominent, nor is the view notably extensive except over a fine sweep of moorland westward. On the other hand, Camp Hill, a little over a mile south, looks thoroughly dramatic, with its lonely clump of pines within a circular earthwork on a 650-foot hill. It is the most conspicuous landmark on the Forest, and the view is tremendous.

This southern end of the Forest thrusts out long promontories towards the Low Weald, and on one of these stands an attractive village called High Hurstwood, quiet, not easily found and full of idyllic surprises, of which the most idyllic and the most surprising is the little church. It looks very much at home in the thickly wooded and broken countryside, but it also looks distinctly un-English. Its design is said to have been inspired by country churches in Italy, and it was built in 1871 of sandstone quarried no more than a mile away. The interior is even more surprising. It is spacious, dignified and full of light. It is also colourful. The clean lines of the stone are offset by blue and gold with a bold blue dome over the chancel. The greatest surprise of all is an exquisite stained glass window showing St Francis with birds, not the birds of the Weald but the wildfowl of the great East Anglian marshes in an East Anglian marshland setting. It is a faithful copy of a window both designed and executed by Mr Harry Mileham, of Hove, for Kelling Church, Norfolk, in 1937.

One of the most familiar landmarks of the Forest is the tower of Fairwarp church. It rises sheer from the heather and bracken and overtops its attendant pines. The church was built in 1881, and in 1936 the tower was added of local stone and the interior equipped with pitch-pine panelling. The village comprises a scattered cluster of cottages, a shop and a pub along a small by-road on the edge of the Forest, but smaller byways lead deep into the heather and gorse where you will find the most venerable cottages, croft-like, low-hung little sandstone places, often very lovely. Fairwarp is one of the oldest villages in the Forest, and Fayre Warp and nearby Notlye (Nutley) are often mentioned together in ancient records.

Nutley bestrides the A22, but away from this noisy highway there are corners and cameos of great charm; and there are magnificent vistas over the wild uplands. An Uckfield guidebook of 1869, referring to the Nutley area, speaks of numbers of little cottages in a valley, each with cowhouse, garden, orchard and one or two little crofts cribbed from the waste. Something of this pattern remains.

Maresfield, slightly south of a heather-covered arm of the Forest, was an important iron-working centre under the Romans. At Fletching, just off the Forest but indubitably of it, Simon de Montfort and his army encamped the night before the Battle of Lewes in 1264, Edward Gibbon, of *Decline and Fall of the Roman Empire*, is buried in the church.

The most dramatic part of the Forest is its northern rim. While the southern side sends out those long promontories, the north falls away so steeply as to form almost an escarpment. Undulating fields, pastures and woodlands reach away below you, across the Medway Valley, to the tall tower of East Grinstead church in the north-west. Lonely pines and birches induce a deep sense of solitude.

Long ago three villages grew up close to this high north ridge, almost clinging to it. The biggest is Forest Row, called 'the Capital of the Forest'. At summer week-ends it is a noisy place, for four roads converge in the village centre, one of them the A22 to the coast. It is quieter during the week, but Forest Row is what I call a winter village. It has the chance then to display its own identity and is not drowned by waves of cars and coaches. Then you discover a definite charm. Not that Forest Row is ever leisurely. With its busy shops and offices it has almost as much the atmosphere of a town as of a village. Houses overlook the little River Medway, which bubbles through a narrow stretch of level pastures.

The remains of a mansion called Brambletye stand beside the river. The house was built by Sir Henry Compton in 1631 and succeeded an earlier Saxon building mentioned in Domesday. Later in the same century it was bought by Sir James Richards. Out hunting one day in the forest in 1683, Sir James was quietly warned that he was suspected of treason and that his house was about to be searched. He turned his horse, rode for the coast, took ship to Spain and never came back. Brambletye, left unoccupied and unclaimed, dropped slowly, stone by stone, to ruin and decay.

Almost four miles east, Hartfield sits in a quiet triangle off the B2110 road to Tunbridge Wells. It is a compact but spacious village, with timbered houses of great age, including the Dorset Arms built in 1510. The church is a little apart from the village but nobody could miss it on account of its tall, shingled spire which is easily picked out from the Forest's northern ridge. The tower and spire date from the fifteenth century but most of the building is at least a hundred years older than that, and some of it has survived from the thirteenth century. You enter the churchyard through a rare kind of lychgate, under the first floor of a small, richly timbered cottage, so that you seem to be passing through a miniature tunnel. There is a similar lychgate at Penshurst.

A.A. Milne lived at Hartfield, and into the woodlands, the glades and the high open spaces of Ashdown Forest he ventured with Christopher Robin and Winnie-the-Pooh, to the delight of us all. Milne records in *Winnie-the-Pooh*: 'And by and by they came to an enchanted place on the very top of the Forest called Galleons Lap.' The enchanted place is Gills Lap, a little pool set at the foot of steep sandstone banks, with pines, birches and heather around and a great vista of heathland beyond. Milne's words are engraved on a nearby memorial plaque on a rock, with the comment: 'Here at Gills Lap are commemorated A.A. Milne and E.H. Shepherd who collaborated in the creation of "Winnie-the-Pooh" and so captured the magic of Ashdown Forest and gave it to the world.'

Almost within sight and not much beyond earshot, Withyham, pronounced 'Withy-ham', is centred more or less upon a small green overhung with trees. Its Arcadian beauty is achieved by the natural contours of the land combined with sensitive landscaping. The Forest begins to give way here to green hills and valleys, watered by the gradually growing Medway, dotted about by oaks and beeches. The church on a hilltop, screened by the trees, looks like a castle at first glance. It is seventeenth century with considerable nineteenth-century alterations. It replaced a much older church, mentioned in records of 1291, but this building was almost completely destroyed by lightning in 1663. A sundial over the porch is engraved with the date, 1672. Inside the church your eye goes straight to the Sackville Chapel, hung with banners, completed in 1680 and noted for the dramatic altar-tomb of Thomas Sackville, who died when he was thirteen in 1675. The whole area is Sackville country. This powerful family first became earls and then dukes of Dorset, and they lived at nearby Buckhurst House, pulled down in 1603 and its stone used to build Sackville College in East Grinstead.

In 1652 an unmarried Withyham lady, Jane Shoubridge, was hauled before the East Grinstead Assizes, charged with being 'a common witch and enchantress, not having God before her eyes, but being moved and seduced by the instigation of the Divill'. It was also alleged that she caused the body of twelve-year-old Mary Muddle to become 'wasted, consumed, pyned and lamed' through 'certaine Wicked and divellish arts called witchcraft, inchaunt-ments, charmes and sorceryes'. The verdict seems to have escaped the records. I like to think the judge was an enlightened man and directed that it should be based on common sense and compassion, and that Jane should go free.

Turning south from Withyham, you come in about three miles to the only town actually to touch the Forest, Crowborough. It excited in E.V. Lucas in 1903 the most scathing language. He found walls and fences covered with placards and complained that 'Never was a fine remote hill so be-villa'd ... all scaffold poles and heaps of bricks.' He continued, however, 'but it is still a glorious eminence.' Crowborough has mellowed since the speculators invaded the Forest, and today its inhabitants are jealous guardians of the wild land on their doorsteps. All the same, we should be warned. The speculators are always ready for the slightest chance.

The western part of Ashdown Forest is less known and less frequented than other parts. It lacks the bold sweep of moorland but in many ways the sense of wildness is greater. You are more deeply aware of the spirit of ancient Andredsweald. Woods and heath press upon small farms, sheep crop the turf by waysides outside sandstone cottages, there are deep gills, whose sides are clothed with a thick, natural regeneration of young beech and birch. Giant and venerable beeches rise above the upthrusting young growth. On the banks of these shaded gills bluebells blossom profusely in spring. Two narrow lanes diverge at a sharp angle from each other in the thick woodland. A stream washes across both when they are a few hundred yards apart. Branches intertwine above the water, which looks leaden on a dull day, but sparkles with lights when the sun shines. Sunlight through the leaves throws upon the banks a pattern of dappled shadows which quiver with every passing breeze. Walkers at either point can cross by means of a small bridge or they can paddle through the water. The occasional motorist has to drive through, unless the stream is swollen after heavy rain, when it is impassable. The place is called Twyford, two fords. The woodlands thin out as the land rises, giving way to clearings of turf, bracken and gorse.

Above the two fords there is a hamlet so cunningly concealed by trees and the fall of the land that you will pass within yards of it and not know it is there unless you keep a sharp look-out. If you don't, you will find yourself at Horsted Keynes, $1\frac{1}{2}$ miles down a narrow road. It is a dainty place of sandstone and timbered houses grouped round a small green from which you gaze twenty miles across the Forest Ridge and Low Weald to Chanctonbury Ring on the South Downs.

The name of this unknown and seldom-visited hamlet, Birch Grove, was on the lips of every statesman in the world in 1963. In June of that year Mr Harold Macmillan, British Prime Minister, later Lord Stockton, and President John Kennedy of the United States, met in the Prime Minister's home, Birch Grove House, a little apart from the green, and there they tried to forge a plan which could ensure world peace. Later that year John Kennedy was gunned down by a hidden assassin.

The conservators face three major problems on Ashdown Forest. Commoners are far fewer, and modern farming does not call for livestock bedding, so the growth of bracken is unchecked and threatens to choke everything else, despite clearance work by willing volunteers. Numbers of visitors to the Forest increase every year; well-designed and well-screened car-parks have been provided at popular points, but how to provide for the tourist without damage to the Forest remains a teasing question. More visitors have brought more damage from fire, and the sad, charred acres are all too frequent despite the unstinted vigilance and hard work of fire brigades and forest rangers.

Neither bracken, tourism, nor fire has spoiled Ashdown Forest. They are problems to be resolved. The Forest remains one of the few wild regions within forty miles of London, and once you are among its more remote recesses, London might be not forty but a hundred miles away.

Now we turn to a very different countryside, gentle, man-made, cultivated, the North Weald.

10

North Weald

The simplest way to enter this region is to go due north from Ashdown Forest and cross the Medway. But it is easier to plan your route if you set out from Tunbridge Wells. In this area the Weald reaches its furthest points north, apart from a few districts north-west of Maidstone.

About four miles from Tunbridge Wells you come to Bidborough, a small and pretty village just touching the fringe of Southborough. It is blessed with enticing views, especially to the high and wooded hills north and north-west. The best place from which to enjoy these views is from the churchyard. The church stands on a sudden hill, so that cottage roofs cluster below. Some Saxon work remains in this church, which is small and built of sandstone with a sturdy Norman tower supporting a little cap-like steeple.

From Bidborough you strike out into a cultivated countryside, cared for and well farmed, mostly pasture with liberal belts of woodland. Pretty villages and handsome houses are dotted about this domestic landscape. Many houses are centuries old, restored at great expense and maintained with meticulous respect. It is a commuter and an affluent area. Men and women who live here and work in London use their bank balances to cherish a loved countryside. They are benefactors to the generations to come. They rank with the wool and cloth merchants who endowed the Kentish Weald with such magnificent churches.

The geological map shows downland to the north and you may expect to find a landscape and prospects similar to the Low Weald, but that is not what you see. There is the same clay belt, but the North Downs are curtained by the lower greensand which lies at the base of both chalk ranges but here rises much higher than the enclosing Downs and also higher than the related ridge south of Maidstone. These big sandstone hills are what you see when you

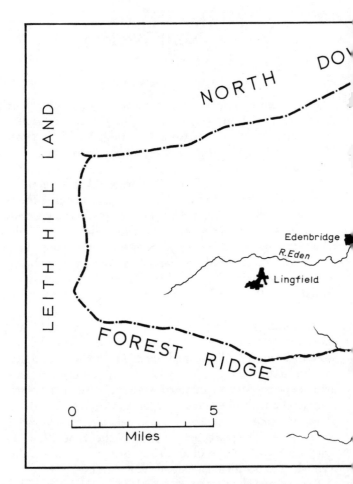

North Weald

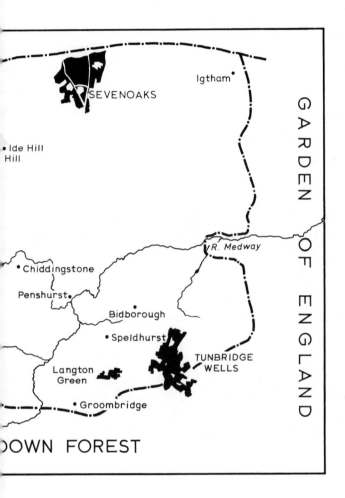

SEVENOAKS

Igtham

GARDEN OF ENGLAND

Ide Hill
Hill

R. Medway

Chiddingstone

Penshurst

Bidborough

Speldhurst

TUNBRIDGE
WELLS

Langton
Green

Groombridge

OWN FOREST

look north as you travel west from Bidborough, very broken, softened by trees and quite unlike the Downs. The clay belt is also generally higher than its counterpart under the South Downs, with more pronounced undulations and much less flat land. You find more similarities when you look south. There your eye meets the high north edge of Ashdown Forest and the eastern end of the Forest Ridge, not unlike the view looking north from the Low Weald.

Bidborough is the most easterly of a circle of villages, all surprisingly different from one another. The first you come to, taking a line south, is Speldhurst, snugly grouped round a large church which at first glance you might well suppose to be medieval. In fact, it is mostly nineteenth century. Nevertheless, you would not have been all that wrong. The church you see was built in 1871 to the same design and dimensions as a medieval church which it replaced. The architecture of the nineteenth-century building entirely lacks the strained effect of so many architectural attempts to copy the style of an earlier age. To look at it, both inside and out, gives you pleasure. So does the beauty of the stained glass windows by William Morris and Burne-Jones.

Southwards still, arriving first at Langton Green, grouped round a trim stretch of grass and almost part of Tunbridge Wells, and then Groombridge, quite uninfluenced by any other place and very much its individual self. It almost surrounds a triangular green which rises to an exquisite tile-hung eighteenth-century terrace. A dainty little church facing the green was built in 1625 as a private chapel to Groombridge Place. It has nineteenth-century modifications. Groombridge Place is also of the seventeenth century, rebuilt from a medieval house and blessedly little altered since. It is not a large or spectacular mansion, but it sits secure and self-confident in the middle of a moat, ignoring the stress and turbulence of the rest of the world. John Evelyn, the diarist, liked it. He stayed there twice and may have designed the garden.

Now we turn north to Penshurst, famed for its great manor house, Penshurst Place, which overlooks broad pastures and noble oaks. Visitors reach it through a walled garden. It has grown steadily through the centuries since Sir John de Pulteney built it in 1341. Sir John was a London draper and merchant and was four times Lord Mayor. The house he built is now the heart of a massive mansion with a 280-feet front. There is a simplicity, a dignity and a lightness about the place which is nothing short of astonishing considering the steady sequence of extensions and adaptations which it has undergone. They continued up to the mid-nineteenth century, and they have left no disfigurement.

In 1552 the house passed to the Sidney family, and two years later that most famous Sidney, Sir Philip, poet, statesman, soldier and scholar, was born within its walls. His life, so full of promise, was tragically short, and it ended far from the meadows of Penshurst Place. He died fighting the Spaniards in the Netherlands. He was only thirty-two. Everybody knows the story of the wounded Englishman who passed a cup of water to a dying soldier with the words, 'Thy need is greater than mine.' That Englishman was almost certainly Sir Philip.

The church is close by, and from the quiet churchyard you pass through a wicket gate into the meadows. It is a pleasant evening or Sunday afternoon stroll among the trees across the grass, and many generations of villagers have enjoyed it. The close association of church and manor house is a common one, the two often growing up more or less together. At Penshurst, however, the church preceded the house by a very long time. The list of rectors dates from 1170, when, it is said, Thomas Becket installed a priest, Wilhelmus, as vicar of Penshurst. Two days later Becket was murdered in Canterbury Cathedral. A stained glass window called the Becket window commemorates eight hundred years of recorded Christian worship from the installation of Wilhelmus as priest. It includes the story of the murder and also depicts local scenes. It was given to the church by the people of Penshurst and was dedicated in 1971. Like the house, the church has been added to, bit by bit, up to the mid-nineteenth century. The arches of the north side of the nave date from about 1200, but a Saxon church may have been established on the site in AD 860. The most arresting and also the most surprising feature of the building is the seventeenth-century tower. It has a squat appearance, but from each corner rises a turret supporting a curiously long pinnacle, and these pinnacles give the impression that the tower is considerably higher than it actually is.

The entrance from the road to the churchyard and church is across a little brick-laid square flanked by half-timbered houses, and you pass under the first floor of one of these, as you do at Hartfield. You see this pleasing group of cottages and church to perfection a short distance down the road where a bridge crosses the Medway. Not far from this point the River Eden joins the Medway, flowing slowly through the meadows.

New and old, timber and brick, mingle without discord in the village, which is a comely place. The villagers know this and take good care of it.

Chiddingstone, about three miles north-west, is equally attractive but in a different way. While Penshurst is expansive, Chiddingstone is compact, centred on just one row, but what a row! It comprises a line of dignified houses in the high street, perfectly preserved from the fifteenth, sixteenth and seventeenth centuries, timber-framed and partly tile-hung, and now in the safe keeping of the National Trust. One of the houses was occupied in 1453 by Roger Attwood who, two years earlier, took part in Jack Cade's rebellion but was lucky enough to be given a pardon. Another house in the row was bought by Sir Thomas Boleyn, owner of Hever Castle and father of Anne who married Henry VIII.

The church stands opposite on a small hill, a big building, big enough to dwarf the row of houses across the road but which in fact does nothing of the kind. Church and houses complement each other. The church is basically a fourteenth-century building, but a fire caused by lightning in 1624 did a lot of damage. It took five years to complete the necessary repairs. No major additions have been made since. The most conspicuous feature of the church is the big west tower built in the fifteenth century, with pinnacles at each corner rather like those at Penshurst, but much smaller. The name of the village, you may be told, means 'chiding stone', where punishment was administered to nagging women. To prove it, you are shown the very stone, a big sandstone rock. In fact, the name is more probably derived from Cidingstane, the stone of Cidd's people.

A broad valley about a mile and a half north of the village holds Bough Beech reservoir, which covers 280 acres. Its placid waters are a tranquil picture with green and sheep-cropped meadows on either side and Ide hill just beyond.

Some ancient houses stood in the path of the water. Usually this is no problem. You just move the occupants, and the houses disappear under the water. But these houses were of great interest and included a magnificent heavily timbered farmhouse called Bayleaf. They were taken down but not demolished. Highly skilled craftsmen measured them to the last fraction of an inch and, with infinite care, took them apart in sections. Then, the trickiest part of all, the sections were transported to the Weald and Downland Open Air Museum at far-off Singleton in West Sussex, on the Downs near Chichester. There they were re-assembled and there they now stand for all to see, almost as much at home in their changed environment as on the green slopes below Ide Hill.

Two small lanes on either side of the reservoir lead enticingly upward into wooded heights, which we first viewed from Bidborough. It is tempting to travel on into these hills, which include Ide Hill, but the temptation must be resisted, for we must now make our way to Hever along three miles of wandering lanes from Chiddingstone.

Hever is a scattered place of few houses and you would pass through unaware of any village were it not for the church spire, which is the centrepiece of a park-like, pastoral country blessed by spreading oak trees and sturdy oak fences. Of the famous castle there is no sign. It stands well away from the road among crowded gardens and sheltered by trees. The entrance is beside the church and looks like an inconspicuous carriage drive, which is what it once was.

Thousands of visitors, many from overseas, pour into the Hever grounds every summer. They come for three reasons. They want to see the gardens; they want to see the castle because they like looking at castles; and they want to see it as the place where King Henry VIII courted the dark, vivacious Anne Boleyn (or Bullen). Hever was her home, and at Hever as well as at Court she received with satisfaction the ardent attentions of the King. Her sister Mary had already been his mistress, but Anne's ambitions went much further. She saw herself as Queen. So did the King, and the fact that he was married in 1509 to Catherine of Aragon deterred neither him nor Anne. Rome refused the desired divorce, Henry broke with Rome, the marriage with Catherine was pronounced annulled, Henry married Anne in January 1533, and soon found he had taken on more than he had bargained for. His new Queen could match his ungovernable rages with equally violent tempers. She had a strong impulse to dominate, loved power and often used it with cruelty. Henry bitterly resented that Catherine had not provided him with a male heir, but only with a daughter. In September Anne gave birth to a child. This baby, too, was 'only' a girl. Henry was so incensed that he galloped off to Wiltshire and to yet another love, Jane Seymour. Perhaps he would not so readily have rejected this daughter if he could have foreseen that she was to become one of the most renowned monarchs in history. Her name was Elizabeth.

With the advent of Jane, the days of Anne's reign were numbered. She was tried on a number of charges including adultery and High Treason, naturally found guilty, sent to the Tower and beheaded on 19 May 1536. Her age is uncertain for her birth was not recorded, but it seems likely that she was between thirty and forty. Anne was a woman of great courage. She asked the crowd to pray both for herself and for the King, 'for he is a good man and has treated me as well as could be'. In those last, awful hours before the sword swept, perhaps she remembered for a few tranquil moments the green pastures of her girlhood home in the Weald.

Ten days after the execution Henry quietly married Jane Seymour.

Anne's father, Thomas Boleyn, who had become Earl of Wiltshire, was shunned by his neighbours and died two years later. Henry took possession of the castle and in 1540 gave it to Anne of Cleves, his divorced fourth wife, who retained it until she died seventeen years later.

Unlike Bodiam, Hever is not, and never has been, a castle in any military sense. It began its existence in the thirteenth century as a fortified farmhouse, built by the Norman family de Hever, who surrounded it by a moat. Sir Geoffrey Boleyn, a rich merchant and Lord Mayor of London, bought it in 1462, and his descendant, Sir Thomas, inherited it in 1506. The Boleyns made some alterations and additions, and the farmhouse took on a greater dignity. It assumed more the air of a fortified manor house with a few turrets tacked on.

The exterior of the castle today is much as Thomas Boleyn left it, a massive sandstone gatehouse, moat, drawbridge and small courtyard. The interior, however, has been transformed. This was

the work of Mr William Waldorf Astor, later Viscount Astor, who
emigrated to Britain from the United States. He bought Hever in
1903 and lavished huge sums of money and much artistic talent on
it. His are the splendid gardens you see today, maintained and
cherished by successive Astors. The River Eden flows slowly
through the grounds, feeding a lake as it goes. Mr Astor needed
more accommodation than the castle afforded, but so that he
should not in any way alter the ancient building, he constructed a
'Tudor village' in the grounds. Hever is no longer the home of the
Astors. Lord Astor sold it in 1983.

The church includes the Bullen chapel within which Thomas is
entombed. Upon the tomb one of the finest sixteenth-century
brasses in existence shows him in the robes of a Knight of the
Garter. Visitors often ask where his daughter Anne was laid to
rest. Alas, even death could not release her from the Tower, and at
the Tower she lies buried.

We leave Hever with feelings of mingled melancholy and
pleasure. The Astors made a memorable home there, innumerable
visitors find delight in the gardens and handsome rooms, but one's
mind also goes back to those earlier days of which the castle is a
mute reminder, and a sense of revulsion sweeps in. To what savage
lengths men and women were prepared to go in their struggle for
power or to gratify personal passions. This country today, for all its
faults, is not as bad as that.

No inn is more photographed than the pub opposite the church,
called the Henry VIII, naturally. That, however, has been its name
only since 1830. It was previously called the Bull. The people of
Hever nicknamed it the Bull and Butcher, and a legend has grown
up that they did so to express their indignation at the execution of
'their' Anne. In fact, the grisly name was not used until 1700; and
Anne was not popular at Hever.

A westward winding lane brings you to Edenbridge. The name
does not mean the bridge over the River Eden, as you may
justifiably suppose. It is a derivation of a Saxon word,
Eadelmesbrege, which means Eadhelm's or Eadwulf's bridge. We
must assume Eadhelm was a Saxon chieftain. The little town is a
mixture of old and new. The ancient part, its heart, bestrides the
characteristically straight Roman road which connected Londinium with Lewes. We have already met parts of this road at

Holtye and on Ashdown Forest. At Edenbridge it became the High Street. The conspicuous overhead sign of the fifteenth-century Crown Hotel reaches across the street to Taylor House, named after Sir William Taylour, Lord Mayor of London in 1469. His arms, with the arms of the Merciful Company of Grocers, are on the spandrels of the doorway. In his will, dated 1483, Sir William left £6.13.4d to 'the works of the body of the parish church of Edenbridge where I was cristined'. The church, a short distance from the High Street, is a homely and welcoming place of sandstone with a wavy and mossy roof of Horsham slabs. A small Saxon timber church may have stood on the site, followed by a Norman structure about 1100, but most of the church has grown from the early thirteenth century. It is surprisingly spacious inside but possessing a quiet dignity.

A white weatherboarded watermill, Honour's Mill, marks the point where the road crosses the river and most of what you see today is probably mid-eighteenth-century work. A prominent sack hoist overhangs a little recess. Another watermill, the Haxted mill, stands hard by the river about two miles west of the town. This mill was built in the seventeenth and eighteenth centuries on the foundations of a fourteenth-century predecessor. Its stones ground corn until 1945. Now it is a museum, demonstrating not only the history and workings of Wealden watermills but also the epic story of the Wealden iron industry.

Now, at last, we turn our attention purposefully to those beckoning wooded heights to the north, setting off up the long, straight road the Romans built. Fields and pastures lie either side, broken by patches of woodland, a scene of peace and good husbandry. Then you take a turning to the right, and suddenly the road grows impatient with the lush and placid land and takes an impetuous sweep upward into the highlands and beechwoods, pausing just before burying itself among the trees to give you a view of astonishing range and beauty, the more impressive because so sudden. Crockham Hill church, farmhouses and cottages, meadows and cattle lie immediately below, and then your eye moves over plane after receding plane into the distant south.

The road narrows and grows steeper, the beeches close in and meet overhead. You are in the land of the charts. To your left are the High Chart and Limpsfield Chart, and to your right are the

The little church at High Hurstwood, said to have been designed
from country churches in Italy

Gills Lap, Ashdown Forest. A.A. Milne called it 'Galleons Leap'

Sundial dated 1672 on
Withyham church

Stained glass window in
High Hurstwood church
showing St Francis blessing
the birds

Chart and Bransted Chart. It has nothing to do with maps or documents. The word is one of our most interesting derivations from Old English, *ceart* indicating a rough common with a thick coverage of gorse, broom and bracken; *ceart* may also be related to the Norwegian *kart*, rough, rocky, sterile soil. The 'charts' were attached to villages, and the villages probably encouraged the gradual spread of a certain amount of timber, of which there was no shortage in the wild Andredsweald below.

Presently the road levels out and then dips steeply, twisting down through the trees, and brings you suddenly face to face with the bland red-brick and gabled frontage of General James Wolfe's boyhood home, Spiers, now called Quebec House, on the outskirts of Westerham. Wolfe was only thirty-two when he stormed the Heights of Abraham and beat his French adversary, Montcalm, in 1759. Both lost their lives in the battle. Both are commemorated through military and personal relics in the house, which is now the property of the National Trust and is open to the public during spring and summer.

You turn westward. The trees go with you. Suddenly they fall back. You are on a populated tableland, a triangular green surrounded by houses and shops. This is Westerham. The leafy, lofty heights look down upon you. Through chinks between the houses you view the smooth slopes of the North Downs. You are on the sandstone ridge, and Westerham is built on a plateau cut into it. Only a narrow valley separates the two types of countryside. The houses follow the slopes down from the plateau, sometimes built into the hillside and frequently with colourful gardens shored up by retaining walls of sandstone. Is Westerham a big village or a small town? You must make your own decision. Officially it is a town; King Henry III granted it a market charter in 1227. In the *Westerham and Crockham Hill Guide* the Parish Council hopes that you will enjoy your visit 'to this historic town'.

It is dominated by two statues, one at either end of the green, east and west. The statue at the eastern end pulls you up with a jerk. That truculent 'we shall never surrender' expression and that determined poise are thoroughly familiar. Almost you hear the slow, growling voice which was instantly recognized on the radios of all nations during the war, and eagerly awaited by most: Sir Winston Churchill. The sculptor, Oscar Neman, has him seated,

Evening view on Ashdown Forest

urgently leaning forward, on a stone plinth which a plaque tells you 'was presented by Marshal Tito and the people of Yugoslavia as a symbol of Yugoslavia soil, in homage to Sir Winston Churchill's leadership in the war'. The statue was erected in 1969. Churchill's home, Chartwell Manor, now almost as famous as the great statesman himself, stands on a hillside about two miles south of Westerham. Churchill bought it in 1927.

The other statue, erected in 1910, is of Wolfe in a very different frame of mind. Sculptor Derwent Wood shows him debonair, stepping out, drawn sword raised high; you can almost see his troops behind him.

The church, a few steps from the green, has grown from an early thirteenth-century structure, and it has a shingled spire and a roof of Horsham slabs. The ground falls steeply from the churchyard from which you view rooftops and then a tumbled landscape of pasture and woodland, quite different from the curving slopes of the nearby Downs. Very different, too, from what the distant view suggests from the south. There you seem to be looking at one long, even ridge, so often mistaken for the Downs. What you really see is a series of hilltops more or less the same height, clustered so close together that you cannot define hill from hill, and you do not see the deep and narrow valleys in between. The best way to explore this land of hills and woods is to walk the footpaths which criss-cross it. But the motorist is not denied too much. He has no option but to drive slowly along the narrow, sinuous roads and has time, therefore, to appreciate the trees, the quietness and glimpses of wide prospects through gaps in the high woods, the gleam of sun on leaves.

By such a route you reach Toys Hill, a little over two miles from Westerham, thickly wooded from top to bottom. There is a celebrated view from the Tally-Ho Inn, set deep in the hillside. At the top the lane becomes little more than a track, and you step from it into groves of pollarded beeches. Then it slides down into a valley and immediately twists and swoops up again, higher and higher through the woods until you come suddenly to a rounded and cleared crest upon which a sizeable village sits, the houses and shops arranged around a sloping green, with a small, nineteenth-century church at the higher end. This is Ide Hill, the name of both the hill and the village. At a nearby hunting lodge

King Henry VIII and Anne Boleyn often met in secret.

Now the road goes down once more, and the trees close in again. In about three miles you are in Sevenoaks, and the great beeches are with you still. Though Sevenoaks is a commuter centre, it retains the atmosphere of a busy country town, which, in fact, it is. The long high street is both busy and noisy, but off the street there are quiet ways and recesses where the din of the traffic is muted. Buildings of black beams and white plaster are a firm indication that this is an ancient town. The first recorded reference to it was in 1114, when it was listed as Seovenaca in the *Textus Roffensis*.

The great glory of Sevenoaks is Knole, home of the Sackvilles since 1566, when Queen Elizabeth I granted it on lease to her cousin Sir Thomas Sackville, who bought it in 1603, when the lease expired. But its history goes back much further than this. Thomas Bourchier, Archbishop of Canterbury, bought it in 1456 for £266.13s.4d, when it was a small manor house in need of repair. He built a palace around it. Others carried out more work on it and spent more money on it. They included Henry VIII and Archbishop Thomas Cranmer, who lived in it for seven years. Thomas Sackville, created Earl of Dorset by King James I, thoroughly overhauled the great palace and introduced a number of transformations, and the building you see today is essentially the palace he left at his death in 1608. It is now owned by the National Trust.

Knole is huge. It covers four acres and has 365 rooms, fifty-two staircases and seven courts. It stands in a vast park where fallow deer graze, and the shadows of the trees play upon its ragstone walls. You could not call it beautiful, though it is certainly not ugly. It does not overawe, and neither does it repel. It does not lack grace, but its architectural merits would probably not be ranked as the highest. Despite its size there is only one word for Knole. It is intimate. Those who frequently see it, or only even fairly frequently, grow to love it.

Upon a wooded hill east of Sevenoaks you are reminded that the Iron Age Celts inhabited areas other than the dry chalk downland. This hilltop is crowned by the fort of Oldbury, covering 123 acres. The first ramparts were built about 100 BC and were considerably strengthened later. But the Celts were not the first inhabitants of the hill by a long way. Remains of two deep rock shelters on the side of the hill suggest that palaeolithic peoples lived here some thousands of years before the Iron Age.

Nearby Ightham Mote is practically contemporary by comparison though ancient by our standards, a complete medieval manor house built in 1340. The 'mote' probably comes from the Saxon 'moot', meeting or meeting place.

We are now almost straying onto the North Downs, and we have also travelled a rough circle which has brought us back to the edge of the Garden of England. We have now to turn back and go west to Leith Hill Land. In so doing we cross the M23, the London to Brighton highway where the traffic crowds as thick as ants on a sunny summer week-end.

11

Leith Hill Land

Leith Hill dominates the landscape in every direction. It is the undisputed lord of the region. The nearby North Downs cannot challenge it. Neither can its two close neighbours, Holmbury Hill and Pitch Hill. The three great hills, part of the sandstone belt which follows the base of the North and South Downs, rise well above the smooth chalk slopes, upon which they look down patronizingly. It is hard to appreciate that once this entire countryside lay under the great chalk dome which covered the south-east.

Hills, like houses, have atmosphere. I have always felt at home on Leith Hill. It is a friendly hill. There is nothing forbidding about it, even when the clouds sweep through the boughs of the beeches on the lower and middle slopes and blot out the view. It has a special attraction for those who appreciate the restfulness of a still winter's day. Breezes do not whisper in the leaves, for there are no leaves on the branches. There are plenty on the ground, however, and when your feet brush through them the rustle is noticeably loud. When you stop, you are at once aware of that special stillness which you find only in woods in winter.

The supremacy of Leith Hill is due not only to its height and massive proportions but also to its beauty, which before the last war was even more marked than it is today. Trees, mostly conifers have robbed it of clarity of line. Its distinguishing feature was its bold, bow-shaped crest. Sunlight and shadow played upon the high slopes clothed only by heather, which in late summer glowed purple in the sun. It would have been intelligent conservation if, up there, tree development could have been kept within more moderate bounds. Britain needs timber, but such spectacular summits should be left clear to the sky and the air. The long slopes below the high land have always been generously wooded.

Leith Hill rises to 965 feet above sea-level and is the highest hill

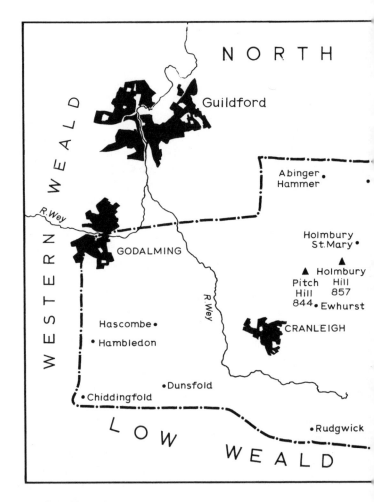

Leith Hill Land

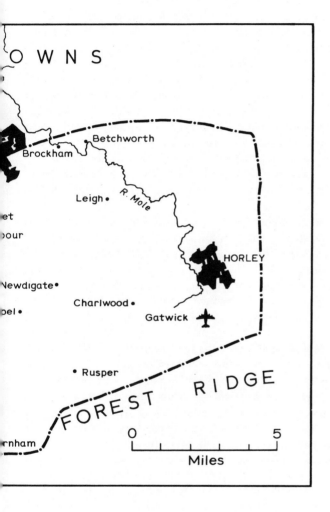

O W N S

Betchworth

Brockham

Leigh •

R. Mole

et

our

Newdigate •

Charlwood •

HORLEY

Gatwick ✈

pel •

• Rusper

F O R E S T   R I D G E

rnham

0   5

Miles

in south-east England. It falls short by thirty-five feet of mountain status, which is a minimum of a thousand feet. But Mr Richard Tull, of nearby Leith Hill Place, put that right in 1766. He built a forty-foot tower on the top. Whether he did so deliberately to make a mountain out of the already impressive hill is uncertain. His main purpose seems to have been to provide a splendid viewpoint for himself and his friends. Today this viewpoint is enjoyed by the public. By means of a spiral staircase you can climb to a platform on top of the tower, from which the prospect is amazing. You feel you are standing in the middle of a compass. There is a tremendous sweep of countryside in every direction, and it is said that on a clear day you can look into thirteen counties, though I have never verified this. Southward your eye travels over Ashdown Forest and the Forest Ridge to the long, far-off line of the South Downs. The early morning or evening sun lights up the tops of trees below your feet.

A lot of people make their way up Leith Hill to enjoy the great vista, but not as many as you might suppose, and those who do deserve a clear day, for it is a long haul. Mercifully, no cars are allowed up the great hill. No road climbs it, no little lanes such as those that wander round it, through trees on the lowest slopes. There are several routes. Everyone is sinew-testing, but what of it? Any doctor would commend it. Besides, the journey up the hill is full of interest. There is an astounding variety of trees. Beeches of terrific stature and great age clothe the lower and middle stretches, giving way to pines and other conifers on the higher ground. Rowan, hawthorn and a lot of holly mingle with beeches and conifers. By the track you will see from time to time a dustbin! Nothing could be more incongruous among these quiet, upland glades, but, alas, the bins are very necessary for, though all practised walkers take home their rubbish, not all visitors to the countryside will do so. They are not the only culprits. Often you will see litter scattered carelessly around the dustbin and you curse the vandals. But mankind is not guilty in this case. It is the deer. They abound among the thick woods and have discovered that there are tasty bits in the strange metal objects, so they rummage and throw refuse about in their searches. Bilberries grow thickly in open patches. In late summer the air is fragrant with the subtle scent of heather and the smell of bracken.

Westerham, from the churchyard

Oscar Neman's statue of Sir Winston Churchill at Westerham

Ide Hill village, on a hill by the same name

Glancing through the trees you may, if you have not previously been to Leith Hill, suddenly stop and stare in disbelief. For a huge aircraft is gliding by on a level with your eyes. It is not an illusion. The plane is making its descent to Gatwick, about eight miles away.

On the hillside and among these quiet woodlands you do not at once apprehend that Leith Hill is not only a little mountain but also a little country, with clear though unofficial boundaries. The villages and hamlets you meet here are part and parcel of the little country, wherever else they might be officially. Some are magnets for tourists in summer, but in spring and autumn they are everything the lovers of solicitude could wish for.

A convenient rendezvous, Coldharbour clings to the hill face, on a sort of wide ledge. The land drops sharply away and the prospect through the trees is dramatic. An Iron Age fortification in the nearby woods, Anstiebury, is another indication that the Celts did not stick exclusively to the downland, though the settlement here may have been temporary, set up by people searching for iron ore. The size, about eleven acres, seems large for a prospectors' temporary settlement, or even a permanent one. It might have been a fort, but a defence against the Romans seems unlikely in such a terrain.

A little over two miles north-east of Coldharbour you come to the most celebrated beauty spot of the whole area, Friday Street, a cluster of cottages set beside an extensive lake with pines and beeches towering above. Trees, rushes and other aquatic vegetation are mirrored in the clear water. Also popular with visitors is Abinger Hammer, mostly on account of the Clock House and anvil clock of 1891. A carved smith strikes each hour with his hammer, and an enigmatic, faintly sinister inscription on the clock says, 'By me you know how fast to go.' The village of Abinger Hammer takes its name from its close association with the Wealden iron industry and not from the hammer and the anvil on the Clock House. Abinger village stands on high ground among pines. Its medieval church was practically destroyed by a flying bomb in 1944. The stocks outside the churchyard were unscathed and are still there in perfect working order.

On a northern slope of the hill Wotton hides itself among the beeches, and at Wotton House John Evelyn was born in 1620. As he grew up, he developed a deep love for both the house and the wild country round it. But though he had an enquiring mind, his scholastic career was undistinguished, to say the least, from beginning to end. It started under the direction of the village schoolmaster in a little room, long since disappeared, over the Wotton church porch. It continued at a Lewes school and it ended at Balliol College, Oxford, which he left after two years with no degree and a vague propensity towards a life of seclusion at Wotton. At school, he ruefully confesses, 'I had been extremely remiss in my studies.' But suddenly he demonstrated extraordinary intellectual gifts and became a considerable influence among the leaders and thinkers of this country.

He travelled widely on the Continent and became fluent at French, Italian and Spanish. He translated works into English from Greek, Latin and French. He developed high diplomatic talents. He was on friendly terms with King Charles II and King James II and he was a personal friend of Pepys. He was one of the first promoters of the Royal Society, of which he was secretary for a time, but twice declined the presidency. He wrote extensively about horticulture and did a great deal to improve it. He laid out the gardens of Wotton House for his brother George, who inherited the Wotton estate. But above all, he loved Wotton, and eventually he went to live there when it became his own on the death of his brother in 1699. At Wotton he died in 1706, in his eighty-sixth year, and at Wotton he lies buried.

He is remembered best of all for his Diary. He started writing it in 1641 but took it back to 1624 and continued it until about three weeks before his death. It had a narrow escape in 1817 and might have been lost to posterity. It was discovered in an old clothes basket and could easily have been destroyed. It was published for the first time the following year.

Evelyn was far ahead of his time in his intense response to beautiful landscapes. Of Wotton House he wrote that it is

tho' in a valley, yet really upon part of Lyth Hill, one of the most eminent in England for the prodigous prospect to be seen from its summit, tho' by few observed. From it may be discerned 12 or 13 Counties, with part of the Sea on the coast of Sussex, in a serene day; the house ... sweetly environed with those delicious streams and venerable woods, as in the judgement of Strangers as well as Englishmen it may be compared to one of the most pleasant Seates in the Nation ... it has rising grounds, meadows, woods, and water, in abundance.

He adds that the distance from London is little more than twenty miles, 'yet so securely placed as if it were 100'.

Evelyn also anticipated the problem of pollution and wrote a book called *Fumifugium or The inconvenience of the Air and Smoke of London dissipated*. Today we would call him a conservationist.

In its entry on Evelyn *The Oxford Companion to English Literature* writes the perfect epitaph. Evelyn, it says, 'was a man of means, of unblemished character, and a dilettante who helped to advance English civilization'.

Wotton House is still owned by the Evelyns but is now leased to the Home Office as the Fire Service College. The Diary, once housed in the library, is now kept at Christ Church College, Oxford.

Holmbury Hill, the central of the three hills at 857 feet has a prospect just as fine as Leith Hill, though you have to make your way through thick conifers to see it. On this hill a narrow, very steep and serpentine road takes the motorist to the top. Up there the Iron Age Celts built another fort, probably just before the Romans came. It covers eight acres.

Holly grows even more luxuriously on Holmbury Hill than on Leith Hill. It is so long established here that the hill has taken the Saxon name of the tree, 'holm'. You also find this in Holmwood, east of Leith Hill. Evelyn paid the holly a great compliment. As a hedge, he said, it 'mocks the rudest assaults of the weather, beasts or hedge breakers'. We are most familiar with it as a shrub, but if left alone it can grow up to forty or fifty feet and may achieve a girth of about ten feet.

The village of Holmbury St Mary, nearly all nineteenth century, lies in a valley between Holmbury Hill and Leith Hill. In 1879 the architect George Street designed and built a church here at his own expense with sandstone hewn from the nearby hillside. Street, who lived at Holmbury, also designed the London Law Courts.

Pitch Hill, the most westerly of the three hills, is also the smallest and the least frequented. Like its two companions, it is heavily timbered, with young conifers planted among mature beeches, but its crest rises clear of the trees. The view from this summit differs greatly from the vast prospect which greets the climber at the top of Leith Hill. Though it is less extensive, except westward, it is more interesting and satisfying.

The roles of both Leith Hill and Holmbury Hill are now reversed. They are no longer viewpoints. Now you look at them and not from them. They are part of the view from Pitch Hill. The rounded shape of Holmbury merges gently into a background of trees and landscape, but Leith Hill thrusts boldly out beyond Holmbury, far into the dappled, lower Wealden countryside, no longer a bow but a giant wedge.

Look west, and a completely different countryside greets you. You gaze down upon the rise and fall of hills and valleys, long reaches of meadow, wood and moor, to far distances where the eye can just pick out soft shapes which could be clouds but are probably more hills, where the North Downs and the South Downs merge to enclose the western Weald. In this land there is music, and up there I always think of the music of Vaughan Williams and Elgar, the soaring strings and the quiet, reflective passages. Vaughan Williams lived hard by Leith Hill, and Elgar was no stranger to the district. Haste should be nowhere near your thoughts here, and also you need to be alone for a while, certainly on Pitch Hill, so that you not only see the beauty of the landscape but also feel it.

The transition from the sandstone heights to the lower land is abrupt. Villages are more spread-out. There are wide greens. You have left the wild land and open spaces for an agricultural countryside similar to North Weald. But you constantly feel the presence of Leith Hill and constantly find yourself looking up to it.

To the south Ockley bestrides the Roman Stane Street, here under tarmac and very much in use, for, as in the days of the Romans, it goes to Chichester. An unusually large green parallel to the road is kept in trim but not manicured. Riders canter over it. It is a comfortable village, with many brick and tile-hung cottages.

From Ockley you can make a round-about tour all through the green countryside, and mostly along the lanes, which lead from one village to another, ending up just below the sandstone ridge. Capel, about three miles east of Ockley, sits on the A24 road to Worthing. Extensive rebuilding in the nineteenth century has not spoilt the church, whose origins are in the thirteenth century. The cottages of Newdigate, some tile-hung, some timber-framed, group themselves where a positive coagulation of lanes suddenly fans out to form a complete circle. At Brockham we are back on the sandstone but not the heights, and it is hard to determine whether the place is of the Weald or of the Downs, particularly as the great slopes of Box Hill rise immediately beyond. But the River Mole which meanders through the village, the pretty green and the cottages grouped round it are indubitably Wealden. The same demarcation difficulty faces you at nearby Betchworth, also on the banks of the Mole, and at Buckland, on the greensand but sheltered by the downland ridge of the Buckland Hills. Here you are almost touching the western outskirts of Reigate, properly of the Downs, like Dorking, though the houses of both towns have crept down into the Weald.

Southward lies Leigh, pronounced 'Lie', pretty and trim, and another coagulation of lanes, and then Charlwood, with a church which was begun in the eleventh century and went on growing until the fifteenth. There are a lot of medieval paintings on the walls, including three kings on horseback meeting three skeletons, but, alas, all are badly faded.

We are now near Horley, outpost of suburbia but with traces of an older village, and even nearer to the din of Gatwick Airport. We shall turn our backs upon them and go south to Rusper.

You come upon Rusper suddenly and realize you are on a hilltop. The views are magnificent: to the north Leith Hill and its companions, to the south a great panorama of the South Downs with a silver glimpse of the sea beyond. It seems certain that the Saxons made a settlement on this hilltop, for the name is a derivation of two Old English words, *ruh* (rough) and *spearr* (enclosure or clearing). Quiet by-roads take you to Warnham, where, in the fourteenth-century church, on 7 September 1792, Percy Bysshe Shelley was christened. He went to a Warnham day school and liked to play round a big lake called Warnham Mill Pond.

Due west now to Rudgwick. When King George IV travelled to Brighton, he sometimes went from Windsor instead of London, and when he did he stopped at the coaching house at Rudgwick for lunch. This inn is now duly called the King's Head, and the youthful face of George IV, formerly the Prince Regent ('Prinny' of Brighton Pavilion fame), appears on the sign. The inn is part of a snug but arresting group of ancient buildings, just over-topped by the sturdy tower of the fourteenth-century church, which contains a twelfth-century font of 'Sussex marble', identical to the material we found at Bethersden. Stone from nearby Stane Street went into the building of the church.

Now we turn north and in about three miles arrive at Cranleigh, a small and fairly new town sprung from the roots of an older village which was a centre of the iron industry. It is a spacious and cheerful place with a big green, a tree-lined high street, a large thirteenth-century church, and a view across meadows to those three big sandstone hills. Ewhurst, about two miles east, is also a mixture of old and new; and here we find ourselves back at the foot of Pitch Hill, having completed a rough semi-circle.

Due west lies the Western Weald, but we are not yet quite ready to enter this land where the heath holds dominion over the country-side. First we shall explore a kind of transitional area, possessing features common to Leith Hill Land and the Western Weald but bearing slightly more affinity to the Leith Hill country. It is a mixture of hills, heath, pasture and forest, threaded by sunken byways from which you occasionally emerge to find a wide pano-rama spread before you. There is a marked preponderance of hazel in hedgerows, and in autumn the broad leaves turn bright yellow, so that the hedges look like flaxen walls.

Godalming stands at the northern tip of this stretch of country, and the heart of the town is the Old Town Hall, nicknamed 'the Pepperpot', because of the cupola on the top. It is not a large structure, and it is not very old compared with many neighbouring buildings. It was built in 1814 and succeeded a former market hall on the same site. Because of its white stucco, it stands out from the surrounding architecture, which is a mixture of many styles and periods, with much dark timber and attractive overhangs. It is the meeting-place of roads, which are mostly narrow and hilly and, alas, noisy with too much traffic. Godalming is a small town but has a vigorous and active life, serving an extensive countryside, and it is not overshadowed by its near and much bigger neighbour, Guild-ford, which, like Dorking and Reigate, is of the North Downs.

By far the most conspicuous building is the church, due largely to the enormous spire constructed entirely of lead plates. The spire arrests your attention long before you reach the town. It is graceful and dignified and is a reminder that the big can also be beautiful. I have no doubt that if Constable had seen Godalming church across the watermeadows, he would have painted it in the style he painted Salisbury Cathedral. It has been there since the thirteenth century, and thirteenth-century murals inside include a graphic painting of St John the Baptist. Here, you realize, is no demure and modest preacher. Here is the fervent prophet, a man given to contemplation in wild places, who will not mince his words. The twenty-eight-page church guide by Alan Bott is a well-written and highly interesting piece of work, and to read it is to learn a little more of English social history.

Through woodland you had to pass going into Godalming and through woodland you must pass going out, whichever direction you take. It is pleasant to drift, relaxed, along the less-frequented ways, and we pull up at a place where trees receive particular attention. This is the National Trust's, ninety-nine-acre Winkworth Arboretum. Here a profusion of oaks and birches grow side by side with rare trees and shrubs. The area is brilliant with bluebells and primroses in spring, and with massed colours of the leaves of many trees in autumn.

A short distance south we discover Hascombe, and what a happy discovery it is. The houses of the village are scattered below two big, heathy hills, Hascombe Hill, with the remains of an Iron Age fort on the top, and Hydon's Ball. Both might have been lifted from the side of Leith Hill. Both are splendid viewpoints. Forestry operations go on beside a small lake, and close by a cheerful inn will serve you a refreshing drink and a good meal.

Further south, Dunsfold strings along a rough common, rather like Ockley. In the church, half a mile down a lane enclosed by oaks and hazel bushes, we find another marble font of uncertain age but possibly almost as old as the church, which was built about 1270 and has managed to remain practically unchanged. It overlooks a grassy valley through which a stream flows, and William Morris called it 'the most beautiful country church in all England'.

Now we make for Haslemere and the Western Weald but pause at two villages on our way, Hambledon, scattered among the oaks and hazels, and then Chiddingfold, centred on a big green, the church on one side, built in the thirteenth century but much 'restored' in the nineteenth, and on the other side the Crown Inn, a big, roomy, welcoming place built in the fifteenth century, perhaps before. Tile-hung cottages are plentiful. It would be entirely wrong to hurry through Chiddingfold. One should stop there and stroll about in a leisurely way. Though astride a main thoroughfare, it contrives to stand apart from the rush and tear of what we call modern life. It was, however, once busier than it is today. It was one of the most important of the Wealden medieval glass-making centres, and it was making glass until the seventeenth century. A window in the church is made up of coloured glass fragments found on the sites of the Chiddingfold furnaces.

A five-mile unclassified road through woodland and meadows takes us into Haslemere.

12

Western Weald

Haslemere, comfortably cupped between two great sandstone hills, Black Down and Hindhead, is the heart of the Western Weald, which is the last territory of the Weald for us to explore. The beautiful name is pure Saxon and means exactly what it says, hazel mere, a stretch of water, or mere, where hazels grow. A relic of it lies on the left side of the road up to Hindhead. The town occupies a high valley, about six hundred feet above sea-level, where three counties meet, Surrey, Sussex and Hampshire. It is a gracious and a spacious place, and it is the natural capital of the region. It is unmarred by extensive 'development', and that is astonishing, because it is easy to commute by rail to London, which is forty-three miles off. Many people do commute to London, but Haslemere is not simply a dormitory. Once you are in it, you are keenly aware that Haslemere is a vital centre in its own right, a place with a life and soul springing from the surrounding countryside, which is magnificent. I think its location and its history have much to do with this. It was once difficult to reach from any point, and anybody with determination enough to get there, come what may, had to fight his way through bogs and forests. The assessors of King William I were not made of such stuff. They 'overlooked' the hostile place, left it to its treacherous bogs and tangled woods, and did not record it in their register, the Domesday Book.

When Queen Elizabeth I reached the throne in 1558, Haslemere had achieved some civic significance with a charter, a market and a fair. The Queen put more power into the charter in 1596, granting the town the privilege of two Members of Parliament. This lasted until 1832, the year of electoral reform, when Haslemere was incorporated into a bigger constituency.

Haslemere remained remote until the twentieth century stood on its doorstep. Something of this apartness lingers on, but that is not

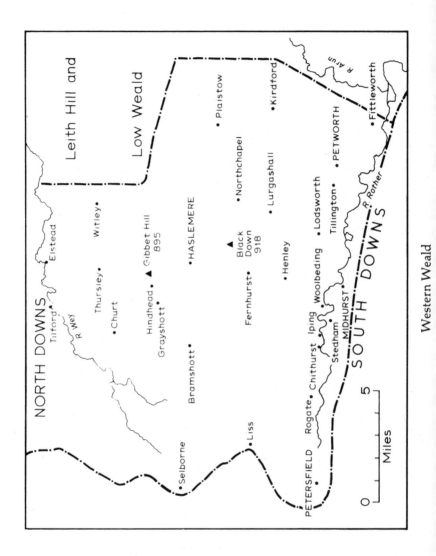

Western Weald

to say the little town is in any way aloof. It is a friendly town and it has a welcoming atmosphere. Whichever way you travel to it, you arrive suddenly and with a sense of pleasure. Stretching the imagination a bit, you feel the subjects of Elizabeth I would not feel total strangers in the broad and handsome High Street where the market booths were pitched. Actually, it is the dignity of the eighteenth century which stamps this lovely street, almost a square. Your lasting impression of it is of steep red roofs rising from sandstone walls, half-timbered walls, brick walls, white plaster walls and walls of hanging tiles, with a venerable chestnut tree at one end, and at the other the Old Town Hall, a rebuilt structure of 1814 with an eighteenth-century look.

Partly because of its solitude and partly because of the district's health-giving qualities, Haslemere grew into something of a fashionable resort in the nineteenth century. The coming of the railway provided an impetus to this trend, which, however, was nothing on the scale of Tunbridge Wells's, development. Neither were the people who 'discovered' Haslemere anything like the smart set which brought fame to Tunbridge Wells or the equally smart set which did the same for Brighton. They did not seek entertainment. They did not wish to parade themselves. They wanted quietness and peace, and they learned to love the fragrance of the pines, heather and bracken, and the feel of the sun beating up into their faces from the yellow sand. The flamboyant were not among their numbers but there was a rich leavening of the famous. Among them were Lord Tennyson, who lived and died at Aldworth House, which he built in 1866 on Black Down, and George Eliot, who stayed a few months in 1871 at Shottermill, on the outskirts of Haslemere, and lived at nearby Witley from 1877 to 1880.

In 1917 a remarkable man arrived in Haslemere, made his home there and gave it musical renown. His name was Arnold Dolmetsch. He was born in France in 1858, studied at the Brussels Conservatory and the Royal College of Music, London, worked in Paris and the United States and made and played early musical instruments. At Haslemere he established his own craft workshops and rapidly expanded the production of instruments, including recorders, violas, harpsichords, clavicords and virginals. In 1925 he proceeded from production to performance and founded the

Haslemere Festival of Early Music. This, now much expanded, attracts visitors from all over the world every summer. Three years later a group of people who loved the arts established the Dolmetsch Foundation to help Dolmetsch in his work. The idea came from Robert Bridges, then Poet Laureate, and supporters included George Bernard Shaw and Lloyd George.

Arnold Dolmetsch died in 1940 and his work was taken on by his son, Dr Carl Dolmetsch. Modern workshops were constructed in 1968, and visitors are welcome to go and see the high craftsmanship practised there.

A museum housed in one of those graceful buildings in the High Street has been described by *The Times* as 'a pioneer and pattern among country town museums'. It could with equal accuracy have been described as a pioneer for museums anywhere. It was invented, there is no other word, in 1888 by Sir Jonathan Hutchinson, an eminent surgeon, who had given much thought to museum reform. At his Haslemere home he established a small private museum based on principles far in advance of his time and a far cry from the conventional collections of bygones. The museum quickly became so popular that Hutchinson built a bigger one in the town in 1895, and this, also, had to be extended and improved. When Sir Jonathan died, in 1913, the museum was carried on by a committee chaired by Sir Archibald Geikie, the noted geologist. It was moved to its present premises in 1926. There, with the benefit of more space, it developed and applied the ideas of Sir Jonathan with even greater effect, delving far back into geological, biological and human history, linking the past with the present, setting before you a saga of continuity. The greatest compliment you can pay the Haslemere Museum is to say its 'difference' has almost gone. Other museums have followed its example.

In every direction from Haslemere except the east you travel into heathland and pine country, broken by small and sparse pastures. You naturally turn first to Black Down, since this great sandstone hill comes down to Haslemere's very doorstep. You can drive about three-quarters of the way up through narrow lanes which wind among beeches and conifers, or you can make your way up on foot along tracks and paths, by far the best way for the able bodied. There is one advantage in going by car: you are far more likely to see deer, probably fallow but possibly roe. They seem to regard cars as harmless animals and may well step out of the thickets almost under the wheels, so drive with extreme care. But you have only to wind down a window or half open a door, and with a single leap they are into the woods and instantly invisible. You know they can't be more than twenty or thirty yards off but, strain your eyes as you will, you will not see them again.

The woods grow thicker as you climb, closing you in, but with tantalizing glimpses of farms and fields far below. Then the woods thin out and suddenly you are on the brow of the hill, 918 feet above sea-level, and the dappled beauty of the Weald stretches far away, far below, with a glimpse of silver sea through the Arun gap. This is one of the finest views in all the Weald. It is not the most expansive. Leith Hill can claim the widest prospect. But there is something subtly different about the view from Black Down, satisfying but strangely apart, and that is more to do, I think, with the hill itself than with the view. Leith Hill welcomes. Black Down keeps itself to itself. You feel not exactly an intruder but a tolerated visitor.

This sensation becomes marked when you find yourself not on a crest or a curved summit but on a wide, airy and heather-covered plateau. It is almost a primeval landscape. The heather is long, tough and tangled, and plentifully mingled with gorse; you may all too easily fall headlong into steep and unseen declivities. I have forced my way from one side to the other of this wild land and it is a tiring and dusty business. The prospects from the edge of the plateau are magnificent. You gaze far into Surrey towards Leith Hill and far into Hampshire to the downland above Selborne. But the panorama over Sussex described by Tennyson, 'green Sussex fading into blue', is the best of all.

Bilberries grow plentifully among the heather, bearing rosy-red fruit in early summer, ripening later to blue-black with a pleasant 'bloom' upon them. The plants grow about two feet high and in many places are as thick as the heather. Occasionally you come upon a brackish pool among the trees or on the heath, unexpected on such a high, sandy upland. Grass snakes, adders, possibly the rare smooth snake and lizards find this type of country much to their liking. The adder is poisonous, so you need to take a bit of care when you sit down. But the adder never attacks and will bite only if it feels itself threatened.

In places Black Down, like Leith Hill, has become too thickly
clothed with trees. They cover most of the flanks and completely
surround the plateau; and they have such a softening effect that
from the distance the hill often seems little more than a slightly
higher part of the general landscape. There are a few points,
however, from which the view to the hill is just as dramatic as the
view from it. There are several such favoured spots on the A283
Haslemere to Petworth road from which Black Down is seen as a
gigantic wedge thrust out into the fields. Clouds sometimes
contribute to the drama of the picture. They scud in from the
south-west, brush the Black Down treetops and float down the
hillside, which they momentarily obscure, leaving a high line of
trees alone in the sky. Then they sail on above sunlit fields.

Four villages shelter under the big hill. Northchapel, cut by the
A283, is busy and noisy at summer week-ends but is pleasant at
other times. An ecclesiastical association with Petworth gave the
village its unusual name. Its church was once a chapelry with the
town, from which the village is five miles north. Separation came
in 1691. The present church, rebuilt in 1877, stands on a site where
a church has stood since the fourteenth century. Bruce
Bairnsfather, famous cartoonist creator of Old Bill in the First
World War, lived at Northchapel from 1942 to 1954, for most of
the time in a former forge rich in black oak timbers. The Celts ran
an ironworks here during the Roman administration, and
glassmaking was practised between the thirteenth and seventeenth
centuries.

Two of the other three villages, Henley and Lurgashall, are so
secluded that it is easy to pass them by, even though you may be
looking for them. That would be a pity. They are idyllic places,
virtually untouched by commercial tourism and therefore free of
'ye olde' and similar inanities. Henley lies deep in a wooded gorge,
and a little stream bubbles through the village. Its houses of
sandstone and timber hold the warmth of the sun and seem to have
grown there, like the trees.

The beauty of Lurgashall is entirely different. Henley's cottages
fit in where they can on the slopes and undulations of its deep
valley. Lurgashall is airy and spacious, with groups of cottages
round a wide green, a spreading chestnut tree at one end of it and a
cricket pitch in the middle. You have to thread your way through a

criss-cross of lanes to reach the village, and you will probably lose your way more than once, but what does that matter? When you switch off the engine, you are aware of stillness, the sound of the breeze in the leaves and birds singing. You arrive suddenly, like coming onto a clearing from a forest track.

On Sunday mornings Tennyson came down from Black Down and went to church at Lurgashall; and what a serene little church to worship in. The Normans built it before the turn of the eleventh century, probably in place of an earlier church, for there is Saxon work in the north wall. A cloister was added in the sixteenth century where parishioners could eat a meal before going home after Mass. This is thought to be unique. It is still there but now used as a vestry and a porch. The lectern commemorates Tennyson and his wife Emily and is dated Easter 1897.

There are two sections to the other village, Fernhurst. One part is grouped round a big green as secluded as Lurgashall. The other part stands on the A286, main road to Chichester. A little church midway between the two was built by the Normans about 1100 but was almost entirely rebuilt in two goes, 1859 and 1881. It remains tasteful and rather lovable.

The countryside around these villages is a mixture of sandy heathland, farmland and thick woodlands. Of the heaths, Woolbeding Common is outstandingly lovely. Its highest point, Telegraph Hill, about seven hundred feet, is only a few feet lower than the hills of the South Downs, here no more than seven miles off; and the view from it is almost as glorious as the view from Black Down.

Southward lie two towns set five miles apart, overlooking the western Rother Valley. They are usually linked together in the mind and in conservation. People say 'Midhurst and Petworth' in much the same way as they speak of Rye and Winchelsea. In fact, they differ considerably, each with its own particular interest and history.

Midhurst is an old and mellow town with an abundance of black oak timber framing in the walls of its buildings and black oak beams inside. You walk in the steps of famous men when you explore its streets. H.G. Wells was a pupil at the grammar school, founded in 1672 by Gilbert Harnam, a coverlet-maker, one of many in the town, for Midhurst was a well-known quilt-making centre. Wells also worked as an apprentice in the chemist's shop which still stands in the broad main street, mercifully free of overhead telephone wire or power cables. Richard Cobden, the nineteenth-century apostle of free trade, was born at nearby Heyshott and was a pupil at the grammar school. So was Sir Charles Lyle, noted nineteenth-century geologist and supporter of Darwin. From 1311 until 1832 Midhurst returned two Members of Parliament. The most distinguished Member in all that long period was Charles James Fox, the unrelenting enemy of the slave trade. He was elected in 1768 when he was only nineteen, and he remained Member for Midhurst until his death in 1806, when he was fifty-seven. His immediate predecessor as Member for the constituency was Sir William Hamilton, husband of Nelson's Emma.

There are two historic hotels, the Spread Eagle and the Angel, both coaching inns. The fifteenth-century Spread Eagle overlooks a large pond and forms part of a group of wonderfully timbered buildings in a quiet corner of the town. Queen Elizabeth I is said to have rested here on some of her visits to Midhurst, and King Edward VII stayed there. In the same group you will find the Market Hall and the Old Market House, both of the sixteenth century, and also the town's stocks and pillory.

The Angel, which fronts the broad main street, was refaced in the nineteenth century, but in the roomy interior you will find more of the fine timber work which is such a feature of the town. The hotel gets its name from a band of the Pilgrim Fathers on their way to Southampton and the religious freedom of America in 1620. These numerous bands of intrepid pioneers rewarded every hostelry which provided them with shelter on their journey to English ports by blessing it with the name 'Angel'.

Of all the noted people associated with Midhurst, Sir Anthony Browne was the most famous. He was also, as we saw very clearly at Battle, by most monastic establishments the most detested. In 1543 Sir Anthony turned from destruction to construction. That year he inherited the Cowdray estate which borders Midhurst, and with it a partly built mansion which he completed. It was the finest country house in Britain, and both King Henry VIII and Queen Elizabeth I were entertained in it, though not by Sir Anthony.

One day in 1793 some smouldering rubbish subtly began to glow. A little flame licked and flickered and then another. It was nothing

Pitch Hill, sandstone hill in the Leith Hill group

much and could have been extinguished easily enough, but nobody noticed. The fire took hold, a high wind fanned it, and the blaze became an uncontrollable inferno. The beautiful mansion which had taken sixty years to build was reduced to a skeleton in hours. A week later Sir Anthony's descendant, the eighth Viscount Montague, was drowned while trying to shoot the Laufenberg rapids on the Rhine. The estate went to the Viscount's only sister. Elizabeth, who married William Poyntz. Their two sons were drowned at Bognor in 1815, and thus, it is said, the curse of the Battle monk was at length fulfilled.

No attempt was ever made to rebuild the house, which retains its beauty and elegance even in ruins. A causeway takes you to it from the town, a few hundred tranquil yards across watermeadows and over the River Rother. In spring and summer swallows and martins skim the surface of the water, twist and turn over the meadows where cattle graze, and seem almost to brush the ancient walls. The large park which stretches away from the house was landscaped by Lancelot Brown, the eighteenth-century 'Capability' Brown of horticultural renown. Much of the park, ploughed during the last war, is still kept under cultivation, and its rich red soil yields heavy crops. But there are large areas where you can stroll at will through glades of magnificent beeches and beside a large lake shaded by oaks, a favourite spot for picnics in summer, a haunt of black-headed gulls in winter.

Heathland stretches westward from the borders of Midhurst towards Petersfield in a series of commons running into one another to form one big heath. The River Rother flows slowly nearby, making for Midhurst in a sequence of curves, loops and wriggles. Five small villages sit on the north bank of the river, which is crossed by an ancient bridge at each village. From Midhurst you come first to Woolbeding, which has a small, partly Saxon church, then Stedham, Iping, Chithurst and Trotton, where the fifteenth-century, five-arch bridge was a gift to the village from Lord Camoys, who distinguished himself at Agincourt. He is buried in the church with his wife Elizabeth, widow of Harry Percy, the renowned 'Hotspur'. They are commemorated by a five-foot brass on which they are shown side by side, holding hands. It is considered one of the finest and best-preserved brasses in the country, like the brass of Thomas Boleyn at Hever.

The shaded lane down to Dunsfold church from the village

About two miles west along the road there is a sixth and much larger village, Rogate, whose church rises imposingly from an unfenced green mound which is also the centre of the village. It was extensively restored and altered in 1875 but something of its twelfth-century nave arcading remains. A massive medieval timber frame supports a shingled bell turret. Sandstone and red-tiled cottages grouped around the church seem to glow with a soft light of their own in the evening sun.

Petworth has no broad main street like Midhurst's, and it is an altogether smaller, more compact place, snuggling up to the high park wall of Petworth House. Many villages are as big, Pulborough for instance, yet nobody could call Petworth a village. It wears the indefinable air and status of a town. Its heart is its busy little Market Square, and it is a flourishing business and shopping centre. Narrow streets radiate from the square, one of them cobbled. You feel you are in a medieval town when you explore through these streets. Here are the overhanging first floors, the sturdy half-timbered walls, the black oak beams. In fact, most of the Petworth you see today is sixteenth, seventeenth and eighteenth century, with some nineteenth century fitted in. But the town has a history going back far beyond that. Domesday Book notes it as 'Peteorde' and states that, 'It vouched for 9 hides. There is land for 12 ploughs. In demesne are 2 and 22 villeins, and 10 bordars with 8 ploughs. There is a church, and 9 serfs, and 1 mill of 20 shillings and 189 ells, and 29 acres of meadow, and wood for 80 hogs.'

A hide was a Saxon denomination of land equal to the area a plough could cultivate in a year. Villeins and serfs, also Saxon words, were people in servitude to a lord. Bordars were cottagers.

The church, on the highest point of the town, is an architectural mixture of many ages. There is no trace of the Saxon church which the Norman registrars noted, but there are echoes of the thirteenth and fourteenth centuries. What makes the greatest impact on your vision is the strong tower. The stone base is medieval. Sir Charles Barry added the top part of pinkish-red brick in the early nineteenth century, and he also replaced a faltering spire with a new one which became a landmark, easily picked out above the surrounding hills, valleys, woodlands and meadows. But this, too, weakened, became a danger and was taken down in 1947.

Haste is mercifully impossible in the narrow lanes of Petworth. You have to stroll and, wandering slowly, you are often induced to stop, stand and stare. Eventually something familiar impinges: you are back in Market Square, with a sense of mingled surprise and pleasure, and ready for a pause at one of the numerous inns or cafés. Petworth commands a high point above the Rother Valley, and from the outskirts of the town you look across two miles of fertile farmland to the Downs. It is a memorable prospect in high summer, when the heatwaves shimmer above the flaxen corn on the brink of harvest, and the Downs beyond subtly alternate from bold curves to soft shadows through insubstantial haze.

The most important building at Petworth is Petworth House. That has been its status certainly since the thirteenth century, and probably long before that, assuming a house went with the manor when Petworth belonged to Saxon lords. King William I (the Conqueror) gave it to Roger de Montgomery. In due course it passed to the warrior Percy family, one of whom was granted a licence to crenellate it. This house fell into decay and was rescued by Charles Seymour, sixth Duke of Somerset, who rebuilt it in 1688-96, and it is his house you see today. It has a frontage 320 feet long, and it is a symphony of clean lines, exact proportions and strict classical discipline. But it is not everybody's idea of beauty. Sheila Kaye-Smith calls it a flat-faced monster. E.V. Lucas says it is like a London terrace. But Cobbett calls it a 'most magnificent seat' and Defoe 'a compleat building in itself'. Architectural writer Ian Nairn considered the front one of the finest seventeenth-century compositions in England.

Defoe complained that the front lacked a vista. 'Capability' Brown cured that. He gave the house a wide, undulating park, dotted about with clumps of trees ingeniously placed to look natural. The park is now inhabited by a herd of fallow deer.

Something of the medieval house remains, including a mid-thirteenth-century chapel and gallery, and in the house there is a reminder of the most redoubtable Percy of all, the sword of Harry 'Hotspur'. This was the weapon he wielded at the Battle of Shrewsbury in 1403, in which he was killed fighting King Henry IV.

In 1748 the great house passed to the Wyndham family, one of whose members, the third Earl of Egremont, was a man of outstanding gifts and vision. It was his taste which built up the remarkable collection of paintings in the apartments, including works by Rembrandt, Rubens, van Dyck and Turner. Turner was often there in person. The Earl was his patron and provided him with a studio. He was also a leader in the eighteenth-century drive for agricultural improvement, he encouraged John Ellman's breeding work on Southdown sheep at Glynde, and he founded the first county agricultural society in England, the Sussex. He died in 1837, when he was eighty-five. His great-grandson, the third Lord Leconfield, gave Petworth House and the 738-acre park to the National Trust in 1947.

Turner spent many hours painting the countryside which the lords of Petworth had done so much to tame and fashion through the centuries. Looking down the long folds of the park, he discovered the ideal focal point to give perspective to his distances. This was the tower of Tillington church. If you meet this tower for the first time in a Turner painting, you will wonder at its un-English appearance, and it may cross your mind that possibly Turner slipped it in, much as Constable slipped in the tower of Dedham church when he felt it would add interest to his composition. But no; that church tower rises above the park wall exactly as Turner shows it. A slim pinnacle stands on each corner, two flying buttresses curve up and inward to support a slender spire, and the whole arrangement looks like a crown. Such lofty flying buttresses are rare in this country. There is an example in Newcastle and another at Edinburgh. I know of no others.

Big expanses of undulating heath lie south of the road between Petworth and Midhurst. Pinewoods stand up from the heather. The South Down are now very close. The countryside north of the road is more broken and more wooded, and you find yourself enticed along lanes little more than tracks to Bexleyhill. This high point is partly clothed by chestnut plantations, but there are wide gaps through which you see big tracts of unspoiled countryside, some cultivated, some more or less wild. Black Down fills the northern horizon.

In this broken land of trees, tracks, hills and half-hidden streams, you find Lodsworth, a long and immaculate village with many old houses, some Tudor, some older, scrupulously maintained. Often a little cluster of ancient roofs bring you to an admiring halt. The church tower and part of the nave are thirteenth century, but the rest is nineteenth century.

You have to look carefully for Fittleworth, a short distance east of Petworth. Commons and woods press upon it, shelter it, largely hide it but do not overwhelm it. Many people who tell you they have been to Fittleworth have done no such thing. They have been only to upper Fittleworth, which is arranged round a right-angle bend on the Petworth-Pulborough road and is approached from the west through a miniature chasm of red sandstone cliffs, sunk in beechwoods. You must drive with great care here, but may this road never be widened.

There is also lower Fittleworth, down by the banks of the Rother, sizeable but often overlooked. A particularly attractive, tile-hung inn, the Swan, takes pride of place among comfortable cottages, and E.V. Lucas thought it 'the most ingeniously placed inn in the world'. Within a matter of yards there are a picture-book water mill and an ancient bridge. The waters of the Rother swirl past the mill and under the bridge but soon calm down to flow sedately through level watermeadows on the last stage of their journey to join the Arun near Pulborough.

Lanes wander casually through thickly wooded countryside north of Fittleworth, where the woods in spring are a glory of bluebells and in summer of foxgloves. The lanes eventually bring you, in their leisurely way, to a stretch of woodland which you quickly realize is different. There is no evidence of skilled forestry here. Fallen boughs and even trees may block your progress, prickly undergrowth may trip you and there are boggy stretches which squelch as you cross them. It is not neglected. It has been deliberately left to go its own way with the minimum of interference. It covers 360 acres and is an authentic relic of ancient Andredsweald. It is called 'the Mens' and the Sussex Trust for Nature Conservation bought it in 1973 for £35,000 and now exercises over it as little control as possible. Its trees are almost certainly the result of direct regeneration of the old Wealden forest, finding new life despite the iron-founders and glass-makers who so decimated it. A forest left to itself is not the neatest place, but it is a place of harmony and balance. So fallen timber decays in the Mens and feeds multitudes of insects which, in turn, feed many birds, including the lovely lesser spotted woodpecker.

You are nearing the edge of the Low Weald, and there is an overlapping of clay and lower greensand. The resulting varied soils support equally varied plants. Oaks and beeches are the dominant trees, but in their shelter flourish holly, yew, hawthorn, crab-apple and hazel. Two rare butterflies live in the Mens, the white admiral, which likes the glades, and the purple emperor, which prefers the tops of the oaks.

Kirdford, about five miles north, sits among trees of a very different nature. You could, for a moment, suppose you had strayed back to the Garden of England, for here you are among extensive orchards. Most of the growers belong to a co-operative enterprise established at Kirdford in 1926. As in the eastern Weald, spring is the time to visit these orchards, for then they are a glory of blossom. Kirdford was a centre for both glass-making and marble-quarrying. The marble quarry industry flourished from the fifteenth to the seventeenth century, but it continued producing marble up to 1880. The church font, dated 1620, is of this marble. So are the floor of the church porch and part of the floor of the Half Moon inn. Glass-making thrived in the area from the fourteenth to the sixteenth century, and there are fragments of the local glass in two fifteenth-century windows in the church.

Now we make our way, still by lanes, to Plaistow, a pleasant little village round a green. From there it is less than seven miles back to Haslemere, where we shall plan our next exploration in the region.

It is a gentle up-and-down road from Plaistow, narrow and carrying little traffic, but the short run is tricky. There are sharp and unexpected bends, so that you have to watch carefully where you are going. At one point in particular, just beyond Plaistow, it is all too easy to miss an almost hairpin turn to the left, and if you do, you will find yourself back in Chiddingfold or Dunsfold. You are helped by the dramatic mass of Black Down, which all the time is either straight ahead or slightly to your left. You cross the A283 and drive straight into a meeting of lanes. Haslemere is discreetly signposted but nevertheless you must take care to avoid the road to Lurgashall. The lane lifts a little, and then, to your amazement, you are on the lower slopes of Black Down and in a few moments you arrive at Haslemere.

We go north into a glorious wilderness of heath and sand, pine and birch. Our first objective is Hindhead. Unlike Black Down, there is nothing lonely about Hindhead. A small town has grown up at the junction of four roads, and a lot of building has gone on beyond this point, mostly residential, with hotels and houses half hidden in large gardens among pines and beeches. Though it occupies a lot of ground you are always aware of the wilderness just beyond. Often the gardens have been designed to form part of the wild land.

The actual highest point, Gibbet Hill, has been left alone, but that was not always so. Once the London-Portsmouth coaching road went over the top, but in 1826 a new road, now the A3, was cut along the flank of the hill some way below the crest and now sweeps round the great glen called the Devil's Punch Bowl.

You can drive up to Hindhead from Haslemere along the A287 in a matter of minutes. Trees overhang the road, their roots clawing over sandstone embankments. In early summer the drive is brilliant with multi-coloured rhododendrons. It is a dramatic drive. The best way, though, is to walk, making your way for about two miles due north from Haslemere along lanes and footpaths, through heather and through woods, to Gibbet Hill, at 895 feet the third highest hill in the Weald.

The prospect from Gibbet Hill is less extensive than the view from Black Down but much wilder. Stage-coach travellers must have been profoundly thankful when this unpopulated, untamed land had been left well behind, and that would not have been until they had come within sight of Petersfield. Highwaymen had little to fear up there. But sometimes the law caught up with the lawless, and it was crime and punishment that gave Gibbet Hill its grisly name.

In 1786 a sailor on his way from London to Portsmouth met three men at Esher. He had money. They had none. He paid for their food and lodging. They journeyed together, and they killed him on Hindhead. His naked body was found on the slopes of the Punch Bowl. The three men were caught at Petersfield trying to sell his clothes. They were tried at Kingston, found guilty, hanged in chains on the highest point of Hindhead and left there to the winds. A stone cross marks the spot where the gallows stood.

It is extraordinary how quickly you leave the week-end din of that road. Threading your way through the Punch Bowl and Highcombe Bottom, you feel you have strayed into an elemental land which civilization has passed by, and this feeling persists when you emerge onto the wider heaths beyond. Indeed, man has made little impression on this spreading, unrestricted country.

It comprises many individual commons joined one to another inseparably, Thursley, Ockley, Witley, Elstead, Hankley, Frensham and Hindhead Commons, with smaller commons intermingling, and then the big heaths west of Hindhead. It is impossible to tell when you are off one and on the next. The total area comprises the biggest area of heathland in south-east England and is much larger even than Ashdown Forest.

Most common land was set aside in the past for rough pastoral agriculture. It was grazed by commoners' livestock but gradually became accepted as open spaces for the enjoyment of the public. The heaths of the Western Weald have never had much agricultural value. Smallholders' animals found little patches of rough grazing among the sand and heather, the heather could be used for thatch, the woods provided fuel, and an unusual community called 'broom squires' cut birch to make brooms. That was all. S. Baring Gould describes these craftsmen in his book *The Broom Squire* and also draws vivid pictures of the untamed country. The broom-makers built cottages among the heather from sandstone picked up or hewn from the soil, and some of these buildings, extended and now modernized, are still there.

There are neat villages in the wilderness. Thursley, Elstead, Tilford and Witley are examples. They seem to have no connection with the surrounding countryside. You feel they are there by concession. You are always aware of the wild land just outside, yet London is never much more than forty miles away.

Thursley is a small green oasis in the heather. Coming down from the Punch Bowl you walk straight into the village street, which, at this end, begins with the church. This is a strange medley, architecturally speaking, but its origins are ancient. Two small Saxon windows were discovered in 1927. The houses are sandstone, tile-hung and timber-framed, and the street, really a lane, opens to a small green, carved out of the heath, from which the land falls away to the expanses of Thursley Common and onward to the Hog's Back of the North Downs.

Elstead is an altogether bigger and busier place, with good shops. The River Wey flows by the western end, where it is

Wotton church. John Evelyn, the diarist, had his first lessons in a room over a porch of this church

The Mens, a relic of the old Weald between Fittleworth and Wisborough Green. Now owned by the Sussex Trust for Nature Conservation

Haslemere: war memorial and High Street

*Petersfield Pond.
Despite its modest name
it covers 20 acres*

crossed by a medieval bridge with five arches. Travellers approaching this bridge from Farnham see first a tall watermill with a cupola on top. It is an eighteenth-century building, but the Saxons may well have had a mill on the site. Tilford has two similar bridges and also a wide green which looks inviting at any time but particularly so at summer week-ends when cricket is played on it.

A few spots have become highly popular and much visited. Frensham Great Pond and Frensham Little Pond, for instance, and, of course, Hindhead. But most of the area remains curiously remote once off the roads, and it is only by walking that you can properly see it and experience its primitive loneliness.

There are strange tablelands like Kettlebury Hill, rising steeply from the surrounding heath and then running dead flat for three-quarters of a mile. Every so often along the plateau you come upon small, round black pools half hidden in the heather. There are equally strange conical hills, like the three in a row near Churt, called the Devil's Jumps. There are sudden bogs among the heaths, often large, studded by stunted trees, haunts of waterfowl, habitats of interesting plants, and favourite breeding grounds in spring for frogs and toads, whose concerted voices you can hear a surprisingly long way off. The whole area is, in fact, a vital reservoir of natural life, but the more so today because such refuges become increasingly scarce, steadily retreating before human pressure. The Nature Conservancy Council, recognizing this, has created a national nature reserve of nearly eight hundred acres on Thursley, Ockley and Rodborough commons. The public has restricted access on the reserve, where you could previously roam about at will. This is a great pity, but the alternative could lead to the disappearance of bird, animal and plant wildlife, often through growing numbers of visitors and the unwitting destruction of habitats.

This abundant wildlife includes two rare reptiles, the smooth snake and the sand lizard. In only a few other districts of England are these two creatures found, and these privileged areas include the heaths round Midhurst, which we have visited. The smooth snake, about two feet long, reddish or grey, is so called because its scales lack the little ridges which make the grass snake feel rough. The sand lizard, at a glance, looks little different from the common

The Moat, a lake on Thursley Common, part of a nature reserve

lizard. There are in fact strong distinctions between the two, but you have to catch them to tell which is which, for the main differences are in the scales and teeth. Sand lizard males are greenish, and this green becomes more pronounced during the breeding season. Gilbert White thought he saw on a sunny bank near Farnham a number of true green lizards. He was mistaken. The green lizard is not seen in England except in captivity. White saw some particularly green sand lizards. Nightjars are regular visitors, particularly where pines break the open expanses, and there they fill the summer nights with soft churring. All through the spring and summer days you could once hear the curlews and redshanks crying, wild sounds which today are sadly few.

Because of the perpetually green pines, you are less aware of the passing seasons here than you would be in an agricultural countryside, with its deciduous trees and changing fields. In the winter, spring and early summer the heaths are a muted mixture of olives and browns, relieved by the lighter green and amber of the bogs, and patches of grass. Only from about July to autumn do you notice any major change, and then it is dramatic: the heaths become sheets of purple and mauve, and everything else is merely background. Though it does not reflect the seasons, this pine and heather country reflects the passing moods of the day in a way that only an elemental country can. It can look bleak and forbidding when a storm approaches; serene and full of soft distances under a calm sky; and a quite ordinary sunset becomes a picture of startling beauty when it throws in black silhouette a line of pines along the crest of a lonely hill.

The heaths west of Haslemere and Hindhead reach to within a couple of miles of the downland, which here is neither North Downs nor South Downs but the stretch of chalkland which connects the two, part of the great massif whose heart lies deep in Hampshire and Wiltshire. Here, the heathland is not quite as broken and varied as the wilderness north of Hindhead, but it is still very much a wilderness. Ponds and lakes are dotted about among the heather, many of them hammer ponds, for the iron foundries flourished in this north-west corner of the Weald. Woodlands are plentiful, with an abundance of birches and pines. An Army presence is not the inconvenience you might expect it to be. On the contrary, it may well have been the means of keeping land open which might otherwise have been 'developed' or enclosed for some other purpose. It must be admitted, though, that army 'camps' are not the most attractive places.

Some villages have been absorbed by the expansion of Hindhead but have managed to maintain their identity nevertheless. Others have far outgrown their original selves. But the big heaths remain the dominant feature of the landscape. There you still find quietude, freedom from turmoil, unrestricted spaces, the sharp tang of bracken and, in its season, the more subtle scent of the heather.

One warm September afternoon towards the end of the last century a young woman about twenty walked up a sunken and tree-lined lane near Grayshott and found herself suddenly on the edge of the heath. She stood still. She had never seen anything like it except in pictures. She had come from the borders of Oxfordshire and Northamptonshire, exclusively agricultural, and she thought that such wide stretches of pale purple heather could only be seen in the far north. Her name was Flora Thompson, and she was on her way to take on a job at Grayshott Post Office. Later she was to write one of our best loved country classics, *Lark Rise to Candleford*. Then she wrote *Heatherley*, in which she describes the countryside round Grayshott with both love and understanding. She roamed alone, in all seasons, over the heather-clad hills, through green valleys where clear streams ran between ferns and mosses; she ventured into quaking bogs, she ran the warm heath sand through her fingers, she bared her head to the rains. She grew to know the heath birds and flowers, insects and lizards. She discovered the homesteads of the broom squires, and she discovered a chain of small lakes lined with trees whose branches dipped down to the water. Even in her day they became a recognized beauty spot. Today they are a tourist attraction. They are called the Waggoners Wells, and naturally, on learning the name, everybody thinks of loaded haywains, horsemen with long whips and horses knee deep in the cool water, taking a drink. The fact is more prosaic. The name is derived from Wakener, a seventeenth-century ironmaster. The lakes were part of his iron-smelting enterprise and one is actually called Hammer Pond.

South-west, Bramshott lies slightly west of the main Portsmouth road, just far enough away to maintain a peacefulness of long standing. It is a pleasant walk from Waggoners Wells. Liss, still to the south-west, has a partly thirteenth-century church with a beautiful south doorway, and then, in three miles, we are in Petersfield.

Samuel Pepys was there on 1 May 1661, on his way from London to Portsmouth, and his Diary suggests he enjoyed himself. He writes: 'Up early and bated at Petersfield, in the room which the King lay in lately at his being there. Here very merry, and played us and our wives at bowls.' The King was Charles II, and 'bate' means something to eat. Elderly country people still use the term. In his Diary Pepys spells it both 'bate' and 'bait'.

Daniel Defoe seems not to have cared much for Petersfield, which he describes as a 'town eminent for little but its being full of good inns'. Most people would have thanked their lucky stars for that, and the abundance of inns should not have caused Defoe to raise even half an eyebrow, for Petersfield was a major coaching town for travellers on their way to Portsmouth. The town's tradition of service to the traveller is still strong, and the motorist is glad to pause there and take a 'bate'. I have myself been only too glad to do so on many occasions.

Petersfield is an important market town of centuries' standing. It has a busy but pleasant square, there are many ancient houses with a wealth of oak timbering which newer buildings have neither dwarfed nor shouldered out of the way. Hard by the square stands an impressive church built by the Normans but much 'restored' in the nineteenth century. There are, however, satisfying sections of the original architecture, including some beautiful Norman arches. Petersfield retains much of the grace and charm of an earlier age and has managed to merge these qualities with the liveliness of today without discord.

The heaths are not far off, and in one place a detached eighty-acre stretch, Petersfield Heath, touches the outskirts of the town and borders a lake called, with unnecessary modesty, the Pond; it takes up some twenty acres. It is a calm and restful place.

It is, however, not the heath country which most commands your attention at Petersfield but the downland, which blocks the southern skyline like a great green wall. Butser Hill, nearly nine hundred feet and the highest hill on the South Downs, dominates the town.

Now we are nearing the end of our travels in the Weald. We have one more objective, a quiet village which has become a place of pilgrimage for the world's naturalists. The village is Selborne. It attracts naturalists not because of its natural history, which is both varied and interesting, but because Gilbert White lived there. White's great fame is due to one book only, *The Natural History of Selborne*. It is distilled from a mass of observations recorded in his journals and letters and published in 1789; 150 editions have been published since. Because of this book White is often described as 'the father of English natural history'.

Selborne lies at the very western end of the Weald. In fact, it is only just in the Weald, and the actual parish boundary extends a good deal beyond, taking in much of that stretch of downland which is neither the South nor the North Downs but the area of chalkland which connects the two. The village is about two miles beyond the last of the heathland, in an idyllic countryside of mingled meadowland, arable and woodland. There are small pastoral valleys with occasional streams, and great cornfields sweep upward on to the chalk and onward into the hazy distance.

Apart from improved roads, Selborne has not changed much since White lived there, which was for the greater part of his life. He was born in 1720 in the Old Vicarage, to the left of a little green as you go up to the church. His grandfather, also called Gilbert, was then vicar and his father, John, was a barrister. When old Gilbert White died, in 1727, the rest of the family moved to a house called the Wakes, in the centre of the village and now a museum run with intelligence and imagination. It has been altered considerably, but here, still, are the rooms where White lived and worked, here is his furniture and outside are his garden and his sundial. There are many intimate little touches, and the one I find the most appealing is the brick path down the garden which White made so that he should not get his feet wet.

White went to Oxford, took his MA in 1746 and then spent fifteen years travelling about England, frequently, however, returning to Selborne, where he was temporarily curate three times. When, in 1761, he was offered the curacy of Farringdon, Selborne's near neighbour, he jumped at the chance. It was ideal. His duties were not exacting and he could live all the time at the Wakes. He remained curate of Farringdon until 1784, when he stepped into a job even more to his liking. For the fourth time he became curate of Selborne itself, but this time permanently, and he held the job until he died in 1793. He was never vicar and he never married.

White did not begin seriously and methodically to keep records until 1768, and he introduces the *Natural History* with a thorough description of the countryside he lived in, worked in and was very happy in. He observed, 'The village stands in a sheltered spot, secured by the Hangar from the strong westerly winds. The air is soft, but rather moist from the effluvia of so many trees; yet perfectly healthy and free from agues.' The Hangar is a long hanging wood of beeches clothing the steep side of the chalk ridge, and you are seldom out of sight of it.

The Saxons had a church at Selborne, but it has completely vanished. It made way for a new church about 1180, and this church has gradually 'grown' through the generations to the building you see today. But at its heart are still the massive Norman stone pillars and arches which support the roof of the nave. Coloured light filters through a stained glass window in the wall of the south aisle, placed there in 1920 in memory of the naturalist. The central figure is St Francis talking to the birds mentioned by White, about eighty of them in their natural colours.

The church tower is a massive piece of work, but it is almost dwarfed by a tremendous yew said to be over a thousand years old. It shows no sign of decay and is twenty-seven feet round the trunk, four feet more than its girth in White's day. But it is difficult to date a yew, owing to the nature of its development, many shoots merging with one another.

White's grave is close to the north-east corner of the church. A simple headstone bears the inscription, 'G.W 26th June 1793'.

From the churchyard there is a steep drop down to a long valley called the Lyth (pronounced like 'myth'). A stream, the Sealebourne, gives the village its name. The path was White's favourite walk. At the end of the valley you find the excavated site of a thirteenth-century priory. Little more than the site remains, but you will find much of its masonry in the walls of the village cottages and on the rockeries of the Wakes. It was founded in 1232 by Peter des Roches, Bishop of Winchester. Pope Innocent VIII suppressed it in 1486.

Another path, made under the direction of White, called 'the zigzag', climbs out of the valley and through the Hangar. You go slowly because it is very steep, with many hairpin bends, step by step, gradually up out of the Weald. The winding path takes you to a broad tableland, Selborne Common, seven hundred feet above sea-level. From this high plateau you look down on fields, heaths and woods, level land and hills, and all the colourful countryside of the Weald reaches far away to the east, beyond the power of the eye to see.

Further Reading

Armstrong, J.R., *History of Sussex*
Church, Richard, *Kent*
Cobbett, William, *Rural Rides*
Cracknell, Basil, *Portrait of Surrey*
Darby, Ben, *View of Sussex*
Gallois, R.W., *British Regional Geology: The Wealden District*
Kaye-Smith, Sheila, *The Weald of Kent and Sussex*
Jessup, Ronald, *South-East England*
Margary, Ivan D., *Roman Ways in the Weald*
Mason, Oliver, *South-East England*
Murray, Walter J.C., *Romney Marsh*
Nairn, Ian, and Pevsner, Nikolaus, *Surrey (Buildings of England Series)*
Nairn, Ian, and Pevsner, Nikolaus, *Sussex (Buildings of England Series)*
Newman, John, *West Kent and the Weald (Buildings of England Series)*
Penn, Roger, *Portrait of Ashdown Forest*
Spence, Keith, *Companion Guide to Kent and Sussex*
Stamp, L. Dudley, *Britain's Structure and Scenery*
Thompson, Flora, *A Country Calendar and Other Writings*, selected and edited by Margaret Lane
White, Gilbert, *The Natural History of Selborne*
Woodford, Cecile, *Portrait of Sussex*
Wooldridge, S.W., and Frederick Goldring, *The Weald*

Index

Southern Water Authority, 72
Spanish Armada, 91
Speldhurst, 150
Springett, Gulielma, 109
Springett, Sir Herbert, 108
Stamp, Sir L. Dudley, 1
Stane Street (Kent), 35
Stane Street (Sussex-Surrey), 119, 168, 170
Stanmer Park, 107
Staple Cross, 83
Stapledon, Sir George, 13
Staplefield, 129
Staplehurst, 43
Starley, James, 114
Stedham, 181
Stephen, King, 92
Steyning, 114, 116
Stone, 26
Stopham, 121
Storrington, 119
Street, George, 167
Surrey, 6, 173, 177
Sussex, 6, 37, 173
Sussex Archaeological Trust, 104, 132, 138
Sussex Trust for Nature Conservation, 72, 95, 115, 185
Sutton Valance, 50
Stutfall Castle, 34
Sylva Anderida, 7

Taylour, Sir William, 156
Teise, River, 49, 67
Tennyson, Lord, 129, 175, 177, 179
Tenterden, 8, 26, 27, 29, 32, 36, 50
Terrible Down, 107
Terry, Ellen, 27-9
Textus Roffensis, 46
Thakeham, 119, 120
Thackeray, William, 56
Thames Valley, 7
Thanet, 32
Thompson, Flora, 191
Thompson, Francis, 119
Thursley, 188
Ticehurst, 70-2
    Roman bloomery, 72
Tilford, 188, 189
Tilgate Forest, 128
Tillingham, River, 14, 22

Tillington, 184
Timothy, tortoise, 109
Tito, Marshal, 158
Toleration Act, 118
Toys Hill, 158
Trotton, 181
Tunbridge Wells, 51-7, 68, 123, 143, 147, 150, 175
    Pantiles, 54-7
Turneham, Robert de, 68
Turner, 184
Twyford, 146
Tyler, Wat, 46

Uckfield, 110, 142
Udimore, 85
Ulcombe, 50, 51

Van Dyck, 184
Victoria, Queen, 54, 100
Vikings, 16
Viviparus Paludina, 1, 37

Wadhurst, 70, 71, 123
    iron centre, 71
    iron memorials, 71
Waggoners Wells, 191, 192
Wakehurst, 130
Walland Marsh, 11, 19
Warehorne, 11, 34
Warminghurst, 118
Warnham, 169
Warninglid, 129
Wartling, 96
Washington, 117
Weald and Downland Museum, 153
Weavers, 32, 42
Weaving industry, 43
Weirwood Reservoir, 133
Wells, H.G., 179
Wesley, John, 21, 83
West Chiltington, 119
Westerham, 157
Western Weald, 170, 171, 173-95
West Grinstead, 116, 127
Westham, 92
West Hoathly, 111, 132
    priest house, 132
Westminster Abbey, 50
Wey, River, 188